SEN.SEI.SHA

An Anthology

Memoirs of the Caribbean Woman

Copyright © 2014 Shakirah Bourne & Juliette Maughan
Each author maintains all rights to her work.
All rights reserved ISBN-13: 978-976-95649-2-3

Sen-sei-sha [sen- **say**-shuh] n.

1. a sensual Empress

2. a woman of wisdom

3. a woman in control of her sensuality

Origin: 2013, island of Barbados, <Latin equivalent to sēnsu, stem of sēnsus>

Acknowledgements

We are privileged to be surrounded by so many great people who have helped to bring this anthology to fruition. Firstly, thanks to Hadlee Sobers, our first Essentualist; "a man who loves a Senseisha", and our proofreader, for his never-ending support from the very beginning of the project.

Special thanks to Leigh-Ann Worrell, who not only helped us to promote our call for submissions, but volunteered to help edit some of the stories. Deep appreciation goes to Craziebeautiful.com, who allowed us to publish one of their most shocking and intimate testimonies.

We have to say a special thank you to our artists, Nicolas Sobers of Ballista! Design for his excellent designs, and Danielle Boodoo-Fortune, whose beautiful artwork can be seen within these pages.

To our contributors, our Senseishas, thanks so much for choosing us to help you tell your story.

Lastly, thanks to all who supported us – whether it was with a soft whisper of motivation, a prayer, or even a Facebook like - we could not have produced this anthology without you!

CONTENTS

	EDITORS' NOTE	9
	FIRST TIME EXPERIENCES	11
1	Picture Records	13
2	Anticipation	22
3	The Orgy	30
4	The Visitor	35
5	My Legs Quivered	44
	COMING OUT	51
6	It's All Right	53
7	Where is the Love?	61
8	My Sexuality and My Church	70
	LOVE AND INTIMACY	79
9	The Story of Us	81
10	Organic Chemistry	88
11	Dessert After the Dessert	93
12	Kissing Frogs	99

	OVERCOMING ABUSE	107
13	Diary of a Punching Bag	109
14	Going Home	118
15	Crowded	126
16	My Guardian Angel	133

	EMBRACING THE TABOO	143
17	Red Redemption	145
18	The Younger Man	152
19	The Driveway	163
20	The Older Man	168
	ABOUT THE EDITORS	175

Editors' Note

Welcome to the birth child of a sexuality and women's empowerment geek and a writer who likes to voice what others keep secret. Senseisha was born out of a need for more honest sexual and sensual stories from Caribbean women.

There aren't enough stories about positive female sensuality, exploring sexual pleasure, self-love or finding sexual fulfillment after abuse. Caribbean women's realities were severely missing.

When we put out a call for stories, we expected to be bombarded with erotica. While many of the stories relay sexual experiences, we are also confronted with the reality that shame, reservation and conflict are a part of a Caribbean woman's sensual evolutionary experience. Sexual freedom and repression co-exist along the continuous and very personal journey towards empowerment.

There is no single story for a Caribbean woman, and we wanted Senseisha to reflect this complexity and provide a taste of different experiences and perceptions, from the conservative to the taboo. This is why we included additional categories like: first time experiences, coming out stories, love and intimacy, and overcoming abuse.

Some stories we could barely read without crying, others we had to put down and reflect on our own experiences, some we had to douse cold water onto our bodies, but the common thread of all these stories is the fact that they are real.

Real Stories.

Real Journeys.

From Real Women.

This anthology provides that space for women to reflect and dig deep to creatively portray the life experiences and lessons, which mark our sexual evolution.

We are humbled and grateful to all of the Caribbean Senseishas who contributed to this anthology.

Juliette & Shakirah

FIRST TIME EXPERIENCES

Picture Records
Lloyda Nicholas

There is a shard of light through a glass louvre window, falling across my face from the bright midday sun. I feel exposed and soiled but I try to keep a brave face. After all, the deed has already been done. There is no going back from here. I will have to stay with him forever because no other man will respect me after this.

I am now his.

But then I saw the flash.

The day had started off normally. My mother had headed off to work and my sister to school. I slept in because I was working the evening shift at my first job out of high school at the University Library. I was only seventeen years old but it felt good to pretend that I was a working adult. These mornings, when I worked the night shift, were the rare times that I had the house to myself.

My mother and I had a fairly unpleasant relationship at the time. I was fresh out of boarding school; rebellious and intent on establishing my independence, and my mother - a Christian - worried about me and was notoriously unable to let her children grow up. My sister was the good one, probably having learnt from the battles between my mother and I. These mornings were like heaven for me, not only because I got the house to myself, but mostly because Gary might visit me in my mom's absence.

Gary was my twenty-three year old boyfriend whom I had met almost two years earlier at a Christmas Fair on my Grandparent's block. My grandparents lived in Linden and this was where I spent most of my holidays as a child.

I was standing with my older cousin, trying to act grown up, and not show that I was self-conscious in jeans that were several sizes too big for me. He came over to talk to my cousin, who was also his cousin, and immediately noticed me standing next to her. I do not remember what he said, but the only thing attractive about him was the fact that he was immediately interested in me.

No one else had ever been interested in me before. But this twenty-one year old man in baggy jeans with hat turned backwards and gold teeth glinting in my eyes was interested in *me*.

He asked me about myself and smiled sweetly, despite his strangely wrinkled face for such a young man, a fact that gained him the nickname "Grampa".

We walked together and ended up on a dark street behind my grandparent's block. I was giddy-headed and intoxicated. I had no idea what was going to happen next. I still remember my heart racing as he turned me towards him, and then placed his lips on mine. I stood there frozen, then he laughed and said, "Baby, yuh got to open yuh mouth."

I opened my mouth and let a thick wet tongue inside. It tasted of alcohol and I inhaled his strangely sweet breath. He explored my mouth and I let him. He leaned back, looked at me and asked, "Nobody neva kiss yuh before?" I shook my head. My throat was too constricted for an audible response. Somewhere in this fog of new emotion, I realized that I had to get home. It must have been at that exact moment that my grandmother sensed that one of her little lambs was about to be slaughtered.

Just as I managed to find the words to tell him I had to go home and we exited the dark street, there was my dear grandmother hurrying toward me. She did not see where we had come from but she instantly sniffed the air and knew that he was the wolf and I the prey. She hustled me home and I was left wondering if anyone could tell that he had kissed me.

Looking back, Gary was downright ugly. But in my fifteen-year-old mind, here was a twenty-one year old man who found me attractive enough to kiss me. I, after all, was the boniest girl that everyone knew. My skin was filled with blemishes due to unfortunate sensitivity to mosquito bites in a country where mosquitoes were rampant. My hair wasn't long and I did not think I was very pretty. Being teased and bullied mercilessly at high school did not help my sense of self-worth.

Despite my mother's assurances, I was convinced that I would never have a boyfriend. I grew into a precocious and outspoken teenager who was often in trouble and regularly in conflict with my peers. All of this, I later realized, was an attempt to disguise the low self-esteem that plagued me.

When I met Gary, I had already experienced numerous unrequited, high school crushes. Whenever I thought about having a boyfriend, it was never with the idea of having sex. Maybe a kiss and quiet moments in dark corners to giggle over whatever all the other boyfriends and girlfriends seemed thrilled about.

But after one kiss from Gary, my sexual desires

had been awakened. It is still hard to describe how aroused I got, just replaying his kiss over and over in my head. I was instantly ashamed and excited at the same time. The Christian teachings that had been instilled in me were at war with the sheer power of a simple kiss.

Gary's interest was not hidden from my family for long. He called to speak to me on the telephone, though truth be told, there was not much for us to say to each other. These conversations were so negligible that I cannot remember a single topic we discussed.

I went back to my boarding school that January, excited and proud to tell everyone that I, yes me, the boniest girl that everyone knew, had a boyfriend. The questions came fast and hard. Who is he? How old is he? What does he do? And Oh my God, the kiss? You kissed him? I realized quickly that barring the kiss, I could barely answer their questions. I also realized that if I had dug deeper, I might have found that he would come up lacking.

So I did what any fifteen year old proud of having a new boyfriend would do.

I lied.

I made up stories about who he was and regaled my friends with his escapades. After all, how many of them could boast that they had an adult boyfriend that kissed better than the men in our Danielle Steele novels. I, the most unlikely one of us, was living the dream.

All of this hoopla came to a head when one day someone came racing to the dorm to announce that I had in fact received a letter. One of my friends had been able to decipher the terrible misspelling on the notice board as my name. I rushed to the board with two friends in tow. The misspelling of my name should have been the first clue that all was not well. I hurried to the office in my excitement and received my first love letter. I saw the childish scrawls of my misspelled name and my school's address on the envelope and knew immediately that I could not show this letter to my friends.

I climbed into my top bunk and garnered somewhere between the barely functional grammar and awful spelling that Gary loved and missed me terribly. He couldn't sleep or eat since I had left Linden and simply could not wait to see me again. He would be coming to my school to visit me during the next week.

Gary did make that visit. I met him downstairs and walked to the barrier with him, painfully aware of all the stares. He begged me to come to Linden as soon as I could. I felt special that he had made the effort to come all the way from Linden to visit me.

That special feeling was soon rubbed thoroughly out when my friends, in fits of laughter, told me that Gary was in fact ugly. I loudly and passionately defended my boyfriend's honour. These girls were just jealous that I had a boyfriend and they did not. I knew I had to see him again. I convinced my mother to let me go to Linden one weekend to visit him. I believe that she said yes mainly because my teenage years had seen the onset of a very contentious and tumultuous relationship between her and me.

I do not know however, if she neglected to tell my grandparents the purpose of my visit or if she told them not to let me visit Gary, therefore deferring the inevitable fight if she had said no. My grandparents refused to let me visit him. They resorted to holding me down and locking the house and the gate while issuing threats if I managed to leave. I screamed, I cried and loudly complained to my mother over the phone but to no avail. My trip to Linden was to be in vain.

But Gary had a plan. He told me that when I was leaving to go back to Georgetown that I should get off the bus at his house, and then I could visit with him and catch another bus later. I packed my bag and departed my grandparent's house as early as I could that Sunday. I went to Gary's house and was awkwardly introduced to his family, who peered at me curiously. He quickly took me out to a verandah area where he had placed a mattress on the ground. We sat down on the mattress and he started to kiss me. My body had been longing for his touch. He went way past second base. I could not believe he was touching my breast, kissing my breast and had his hand in my underwear. I felt like I was being ravished and I loved every minute of it. I had enough presence of mind to stop him from going further than that, but I returned to Georgetown that day feeling slightly dirty.

Over the next year, Gary visited me at home with my mother reluctantly accepting him as my boyfriend. She reasoned that if she maintained the rule that he could only visit when she was at home, then I would remain undeflowered.

But she could not stand the sight of him. Her dislike was barely concealed and she probably was hoping it was just a phase. You see, I had learned that not only could Gary not string together a proper sentence, but he was also chronically unemployed. He was what my mother called a "No good". Yet I persevered with him mainly because he liked me and I loved the attention.

Gary began to plan his visits to coincide with my night shifts, which would mean that I would be home alone in the morning.

This day he meant business.

He took my arm and said, "Is over ah whole year I waiting. Yuh is a big gurl now. Yuh wukking and thing. Is time I get this thing." I went with him walking like a man going to the gallows, but another part of me rationalised that he was right. It was time. I was resigned to it.

There was nothing romantic about it. He undressed me, touched me a little, then attempted to insert his penis. Do I sound a little clinical? Well that is because this is how it suddenly felt.

His penis, I later discovered by comparison, was above average in size, and by above average, I mean it was huge! He started off slowly at first but soon lost patience with my crying, squirming and constant appeals for him to stop because it was hurting so badly. At this point he held me down and forced his way inside me.

I screamed involuntarily. It felt like someone was ripping my insides apart. It was brutal and excruciatingly painful, and just like that, it was done. I was no longer a virgin and suddenly I realized that I had lost something valuable. To make matters worse, the neighbour's son, who had probably heard my screams and knew what was happening, started to laugh loudly in the quiet still of the midday sun.

There I lay, sullied and soiled. No longer pure and untouched, but now like any other girl. It is funny that I never realized how special my virginity was to me until that moment. Gary, for his part, seemed pleased. He inspected the bloodstain on the sheet as I got dressed and smiled proudly. I thought to myself, "He has taken this valuable thing from me. He will never leave me." I got up gingerly and dressed, hoping for some affection from him. I was feeling raw, physically and emotionally.

I tried to smile through the humiliation I felt in that moment as I made my way to the living room and lay down in the chair. And that is when it happened.

I saw the flash.

Gary had removed a camera from the baggy jeans of his pocket and taken my picture. "This is fuh meh records," he said.

That afternoon as we were leaving the house, he for home and me for work, he walked so fast I could hardly keep up with him. It felt like he did not want to be seen walking with me.

Gary's visits to Georgetown ceased after that day. On my next visit to Linden he told me that he wasn't interested in the relationship anymore. I was humiliated. I begged him to take me back, because in my head, I did not want to be the one to be dumped. I just wanted him to take me back so that I could then turn around and be the one to say goodbye. He never gave in.

My shame was complete.

This, my first sexual experience, left me feeling soiled and discarded. In future relationships I would be quick to allow it to become physical because I told myself, "What's the point? It's not like I'm a virgin anymore." I began to place heavy value on guys who would not break up with me. Even if they treated me badly, I just wanted to be with someone who would not discard me. A man who walked too quickly when he walked with me in public though, was a red flag.

As I grew older, I often made mistakes in relationships based mainly on my lack of self-worth. Gary was only the first of many moments when I let a man treat me as lowly as I saw myself, but over time I have grown up and learnt to love myself.

As I grew wiser, I came to understand that self-love is the key to the empowerment of girls and women, especially with regard to sexuality and relationships.

Anticipation
Cher Corbin

The fasten seat belt sign was illuminated, causing a scurry through the cabin by passengers who were lounging around, stretching their legs after the last meal service on the four-hour flight. Fifteen more minutes and we would be landing.

I followed the flight attendant's instructions and then reached for my compact mirror to perform my version of the landing preparations. Two anxious brown eyes were reflected as I dabbed my nose and cheeks with powder. My heightened state was not due to any fear of flying or landing for that matter, but the thought of knowing that I would soon come face to face with a dream, a fantasy that would embody my wildest desires. I exhaled and immediately felt a dull upward thud, the reverse thrust of the Boeing 757.

I was blessed. Having worked tirelessly over the years, overcoming ridicule, self-doubt and insecurities, I was now at the pinnacle of my profession. I travelled quite frequently and the month of May usually found me in one island or the other, presenting papers and having discussions with my colleagues.

The announcement for the annual general meeting for law enforcement consultation arrived at my office by courier and the information contained was quite comprehensive, except for the small matter of the accommodation rates. There was a contact name and number at the bottom of the communication, so I immediately decided to make the call.

"Good morning, can I be of assistance?" A smooth mix of the Queen's English spiced with Jamaican twang floated through the earpiece. I immediately touched my chest to quell the illogical heaving of my breasts.

"Ammmm…yes, I was trying to get some clarification on the hotel special rate for the conference and also to make a booking. Would you be able to help me?"

Well, he certainly did help me. I am not sure if I got all the information I needed but I sure as hell got the feel of something. By the time the call had ended I headed straight for the bathroom.

Recently separated and having to juggle the newly acquired responsibilities of single parenthood whilst suffering the stinging residual pain of a failed marriage, I subconsciously needed attention. I got that and then some.

The text messages started right away – innocently enough at first and then everything changed, drastically. Simple keystrokes transformed into emotive charges that flared shockingly on both ends. The week before my departure, I found it very difficult to focus and concentrate on my daily tasks. I had seemingly perfected the art of daydreaming.

"Send me a photo of yourself, Baby Girl," he pleaded. "I am sure the sweet honey I hear in your voice can't compare to the awesome beauty of your smile."

Gosh! Just reading those words sent a fluttering straight to the goddess cup that held my sacred joy. My heart raced and my fingers became clammy. I laid the Blackberry on the table while I typed.

"I don't know if I should..."

But I did anyway. The floodgates were released and all inhibitions were thrown to the wind.

Have you ever experienced interacting with a person without physical contact, without preconceived notions or ideas, without judgment? Do you know how it feels? Well I do!

Absolute Freedom!

We texted at least six times a day, we savoured the minutes in between meetings; the call-backs and the sound-bites, the suggestions and the role playing. It didn't matter what time it was, it didn't matter where we were. His words were simple but effective. The flutter in my belly, the shivering of my groin, the dampness of my...

"Ladies and Gentlemen, welcome to Jamaica!" The usual announcements followed and then... *"Would Ms Corbin please identify herself at the front of the plane on disembarking?"*

I was a bit startled at the notification and inhaled deeply. I moved to the front of the cabin and as I stepped onto the jet bridge, I saw him.

Time slowed down. My heart rate sped up and I could hear the blood pumping in my ears. My mouth tasted like chalk, and I licked my lips. He was fairly tall and of average build but what startled me was his skin; it was the colour of dark Ghirardelli Chocolate. Clean-shaven with a low military haircut, he stood at ease; hands on hips pushing his sports coat aside, with a controlled, slightly stern look on his face. I beckoned to the flight attendant and identified myself. She in turn directed me to the tall dark stranger and as I turned to him, our eyes met for the first time.

He smiled.

"Ms Corbin? Hi, I am Chante, Chante Christopher."

I attempted to exude confidence but knew that I was failing miserably. I extended my hand in greeting and then it happened. His grasp was like fire and ice at the same time. I caught my breath and my left knee gave way. *What the hell!*

He caught me before I could fall and this brought me close to his chest. It was heaving.

Time stopped.

I could hear his breathing as his mouth was close to my ear. His cologne was light, like Cool Waters, but there was still a trace of his manly scent. *Wake up girl! Wake up!* I pulled away from him, a bit self-consciously and I laughed awkwardly. "I am so sorry. Clumsy me."

"Not at all." He smiled a warm, comforting smile that completely changed the landscape of his face. He then took my carry-on and ushered me through immigration, customs and on to the arrival hall.

A dark blue sedan was waiting at the curb. Chante opened the left passenger back door for me and held my hand as I got in. He held it a little too long and I felt flushed as he gently rubbed his thumb across the back of my palm. His eyes were barely visible behind his sunglasses but I could tell that his gaze was fixed on me.

As I settled into the back seat and he in the front, I closed my eyes and tried to slow my breathing. The cabin in the sedan although spacious, seemed almost too small, claustrophobic even. I caught the driver's eye in the rear view mirror and he raised his eyebrows at me. I ignored him because I would not be the object of his amusement; I could imagine what he was thinking.

My phone vibrated.

"Hey Baby Girl…you finally here…God I can't wait to hold you."

I whimpered and the driver looked my way again. I countered with a scowl. I responded, "me too…"

I felt the vibrations constantly for the next twenty minutes as we drove into town. It was getting dark, and feeling the plush leather of the seat envelop me, I blocked everything out and focused on the smooth words of my virtual lover. Suddenly, there was a warm touch on my ankle. Chante had somehow inconspicuously placed his hand behind his front seat to caress my skin.

Oh my goodness, thank God for panty liners.

By the time we got to the hotel, I could feel the dampness creeping down my thighs. I am certain I left a telltale spot on the leather.

Chante assisted with my check-in and his resident charm was obviously not lost on the young lady at the front desk. She was batting her eyelids and licking her lips to the point that I was getting quite irritated by the posturing. *He's mine, Bitch.*

When the transaction was completed, Chante steered me away from the other guests who were arriving and handed me the room key.

"Thank you for your help. I guess I will see you in the morning." I was unsure whether I had just made a statement or asked a question.

He gave me the room key, leaned forward and kissed me on my cheek. He whispered, "I will see you later. Keep it warm for me."

The tingle on my face spread down my back and made its way to the base of my spine. Reaching around him I pressed the button for the elevator.

"Don't take too long," I replied in my most come-hither voice. He was smiling as the elevator doors closed and I collapsed in the corner of the glass-lined box.

Oh shit! This was not happening.

It was now close to eight o'clock at night and I was too nervous to eat dinner, so I made a cup of tea and finished the sandwich I had purchased some six hours before. It didn't have any taste but I didn't care. He hadn't called and there were no messages on my phone.

I chided myself aloud. "This is ridiculous! I don't know this man from Jack. Why I am having all of this anxiety. My belly hurts, my breasts hurt, my vee-jay-jay is…." The room phone rang.

"Good evening, Ms Corbin, I have a call for you. Connecting you now." The operator went off the line.

"Hi, honey…" The smooth sweet sound of his voice bathed me in warmth, head to toe and all between. "I am so sorry I didn't call earlier. I got caught up with another meeting with my boss and I left my phone in the car."

I exhaled. OK, so he had a good reason. I wasn't being stood up after all then. I decided to play it cool. "No problem, Chante, it's fine. I understand."

"Do you want me to still come over? I get off at midnight and I could be there before one. I want to taste you so badly." His timbre lowered significantly and I squirmed on the edge of the bed.

"Yes, yes. Please come."

"That I will," he replied, "again and again and again."

The phone line went dead.

I lay on the bed with the phone receiver in my hand. I couldn't move, couldn't think. The constant beeping of the unit brought me back to reality. Turning to my left, I looked at the digital clock on the bedside table. I'd been lying there for an hour. It was just going on nine. I decided to take a shower and prepare myself; for what I was not sure.

Admittedly the hot shower loosened my stiff muscles and relaxed my on-edge nerves. Drying off and loosening my hair from the up sweep, I took the time to layer on copious amounts of the scented body lotion I had purchased on leaving the airport back home; neck, arms, under and between breasts, behind knees, inside thighs and just on the outer edges of my newly shaved vulva.

Hmmm, the chilled cream felt marvellous against my warm skin. I wondered if he would head south. I had always wanted to experience it. You know what I mean: getting eaten, muff diving, whatever you call it.

Thinking about it, I lay back on the cool pillows and closed my eyes. The AC-unit in the room expelled a steady stream of chilled air over my naked body. My breasts tightened and my nipples became erect. I shifted on the sheets and the material rose between my legs as I rolled onto my stomach.

Bliss, that's what it was. Anticipation – yes, I remembered a poem I had read in an anthology recently. Funny how I could remember every single word:

>*her eyes sparkled*
>*clear luminescent globes*
>*searching*
>*craving*
>*the object of her desire*
>*her lips tingled*
>*and parted*
>*moistened*
>*patience*
>*patience - sweet rosebud*
>*he will come soon*
>*very soon*

she smiles
knowing the bliss
that will envelop her whole being
fray her every nerve
touch her inner sanctum
is on its way

she smiles
knowing finally
connection
heat
aching
shivering
anticipation

she smiles
she is ready

There is a knock on the door. I looked at the clock. It was 12.45pm. I must have fallen asleep. The knock was soft but persistent. A low, husky voice beckoned, "Baby girl, it's me."

I rolled off the bed.

He did come.

I opened the door. Standing face to face with my fantasy, my desire, I bared it all.

I was ready.

Yes, I was ready.

The Orgy
V.I.P

"Hold my phone for me. If I am not back in 15 minutes, come get me."

We exchange nervous looks before she disappears inside the house. I stare at the neon green numbers that illustrate the time on my friend's cell phone, counting down the minutes and shaking my head. I had promised her a low-key night; a couple of drinks at a small bar on the coast with a few acquaintances and then back home. I apologised profusely as we departed because there was nothing fun and exciting going on...or so I thought.

It was a cool lime. We went to a bar that neither of us had been to before, and we had one too many. The night started off a bit slow, but then the barman turned up the music and as if on cue, the alcohol and sweet soca rhythms took hold. Soon we were all gyrating frantically to the beat; one woman bent over the bar chair pooching back on a guy; another couple making their way down to the ground, whilst others flittered about, rubbing themselves on limbs and posteriors as they made their way around the tiny bar. By the time the bar was ready to close, we were now fully charged and wanting more.

We all decided on an "after party" and one of the guys, hands in air announced, "Everybody, party by me!" As we went about settling the bill, my friend whispered that she would be back. I watched her make her way towards the exit of the bar where she stopped to talk to a couple that were a part of our group. Sly and flirtatious smiles crossed their lips and my friend stood there listening to them with a mix of shyness and awe…

01:37hrs

Only five minutes have passed. I peer into the house again before striking up an arbitrary conversation about nothing in particular with a guy sitting on the outside porch. He appears to be neither here nor there and I suspect that he is just as confused as I am about why we agreed to continue the night with an "after party" at our mutual friend's apartment. Coming from the previously charged environment, the switch to one with no music was sapping my mood. I smile and feign an attentive ear whilst trying not to look too guilty or distracted.

How did a few drinks on a quiet night end up with such an indecent proposal?

I pour myself another rum and coke from the minibar set up at my side.

01:47hrs

I refresh my email another five times and check Facebook and Twitter for updates just to pass the time. I give up and decide that simply watching the minutes go by may calm my nerves and try to focus on finishing my drink. Surely she would have screamed by now if she weren't safe.

Two minutes later I find myself outside of the closed bedroom door, phone in hand, trying to decide whether to knock or just barge in. I slowly turn the knob, crack the door and slide quietly into the room, closing the door behind me.

It is pitch black and it takes a few seconds for my eyes to adjust to the darkness. Even then, I can make out the silhouettes of three bodies merged into one. I pause, half expecting that they would all look up in horror and that I would have to explain myself, but the activity continues.

I quickly realise that my friend is the main course.
I press the button to activate the phone's dim light and quickly search for her face.

Our eyes meet and I stifle a giggle as she silently mouths the words, "Oh my God!" over and over again. A woman lies between her thighs whilst the male partner devours the top half of her naked body. I go to her side and ask if she is ok. In the awkwardness of the moment I try to return her cell phone, which she refuses. I make a beeline for the door.

But between the bed and the exit my feet fail me and I can only manage to perch myself up against the wall by the bedroom door. Maybe it is the collective sounds of oral pleasure, or perhaps it is the arbitrary and appreciative commentary between the couple over the taste, feel and scent of their willing prey. Whatever it is, I realise that whilst part of me wanted to be respectful and leave, the other half very much wanted to stay. With my back pressed firmly against the opposite wall, I stand motionless, fixated by the image before me.

I am startled by a flood of light, quickly followed by darkness again as a fifth figure - a male - enters the room. As if on cue, he takes his place at the foot of the bed. My eyes dart over to where he stands. I watch him as he takes the hand of the other man and leads him into a seated position in front of him. Not wanting to waste another second, the newcomer drops to his knees and places an erect and throbbing penis into his hungry mouth.

I am lost in the visual of the involuntary contortion

of a masculine face in ecstasy. This injection of added testosterone increases the sexual charge in the room and I watch as drawn lips and cheeks firmly and expertly consume the head, and then move all the way down to the base of a perfect, erect cock. My mouth salivates and I lick my lips trying to imagine the taste.

I am so spellbound by this novel image of two men that I don't realise that someone is now perched beside me. Our eyes meet and we share a quick smile before returning our gaze to centre stage, neither of us wanting to miss any part of the action. Another person enters and then another. Each dives in, climbing over and under legs and arms with female and male erogenous zones as their targets.

The air is thick and heavy, reminding me of the days making out in the back seat of an old Suzuki on a hot summer's night - windows up, everything foggy, sweat dripping everywhere.

I am wet.

My focus returns to the human pile on the bed – two women amongst a number of gorgeous men. Lips everywhere – against other lips, on inner thighs, sucking on earlobes or expertly navigating intimate spaces with no discrimination.

Hands lost in moist places, caressing curves and rock hard abs. This is a place that I had never been before – so open, so carefree.

I scan the scene again and stop at the tall, dark and lean body of one of the men being kissed and caressed all over by multiple lips and hands. Our eyes meet and a wicked smile registers across his lips.

My nipples get harder.

He is just my type and for a moment I imagine

myself mounting and riding him to orgasm.

I am distracted by the crescendo building up in the far corner of the room, low at first but sounds increasingly escape an open mouth as climax approaches. Soft giggles follow and the group momentum continues. I close my eyes, taking the moment in.

A hand clasps mine and I feel myself being led towards the bed by Mr Tall, Dark & Handsome.

It is now or never.

My body is hungry to be touched and to experience unexplored fantasies of group sex but in the short distance between the wall and the bed, the spell is broken. My mind is not having it. I pull away and flee the room, straight out through the front door into the cool air of the night. With deep breaths I take in all that transpired. Why did I stay? Why did I run away? My head is still swirling from that familiar cocktail effect of rum and sexual tension.

Moments later, one by one, persons begin exiting the room and my friend walks up to me with a surprised look. Evidently she is still in disbelief and apparently so am I.

On the way home my friend and I are each in our own thoughts. She makes a comment about how wild and spontaneous the night was, which sparks an animated and detailed recount of the night. We arrive at her home and I bid her goodnight. She makes me promise to take her out for another "boring night".

On my way home, I smile and remember a tagline from one of my favourite films, "Voyeurism is participation."

I can't wait to get home and relive the experience all on my own.

The Visitor
Tam Brann

I had only learned to ride a bike three years ago. Common Entrance was around the corner, but my breasts weren't. They were no blossoming summits; no bulbous parts for me to heave toward my chin and show off like the other girls my age in school.

Instead, my nipples fell flat like raisins against my chest. My "figure one" appearance didn't appeal to any peers of the opposite sex and I was crucified by everyone for my boyish looks and behaviour. Everyone called me Mitch as if I were a boy; ignoring the name my parents gave to me - Michelle. They laughed at me and I felt hurt but I put on a good face, acting as if I didn't care about what any of them said. I liked my life…until she barged in.

In the early morning, a warm sensation tickled between my legs. It cut my sweet sleep short. My fingers ran through this wetness, which was now cold and sticky. It came as fresh as the first day, but somehow, she didn't want me to keep her a secret. She snuck into my sleep, gutting my insides with her rusty, metallic scent.

I hauled the sheets off my bed, and forced them in the sink along with my nightclothes, underwear and a washrag. Then I dumped the bleach on top and filled the sink with water. The strong scent filled my nostrils causing my eyes to water. But, my eyes too were filled with the shame of this unexpected visitor. I wanted to bleach away the stain causing my pain. It was as if she didn't want to leave. Yes, that good-for-nothing held on for as long as she could and dragged the colour from the sheet, underwear and washrag, too. I watched her fade, disappear in a reluctant, half-hearted manner from my cobalt, cotton panties and baby yellow sheets.

"What are you doing?" Mummy shouted from behind me.

I hated two things. One: an ambush where I'm caught off-guard and can't gather myself to respond, and two: when I'm doing something in private and someone sneaks up on me. There was always a battle between my heart and chest, my mind and body, and I often found that I couldn't function.

It was difficult trying to process my mother's barraging questions. She was like a shark, sniffing for the very life-giving blood that I despised.

"What are you doing in here with bleach?" She peered over my shoulder and dragged the bottle out of my hand.

"Nothing." I bowed my head feeling ashamed.

"Open up the place." Mummy shoved me aside and pushed the bathroom windows up. She paused over the sink.

"Wait, those are my good sheets. She closed her eyes and sighed at the ugly, faded mess. She held her sheets in front of my face. The water dripped onto the floor in a manner that made me want to drip into nothingness like the rain. "What's wrong with you?"

I froze – didn't know what to say. I could see the neighbour bustling about in her kitchen, which was directly opposite our bathroom window.

"What is that?" Mummy's voice was so loud that Minelva, our neighbour, stopped what she was doing. We caught her looking through her window and listening. She jerked her head back and began to potter about again.

"Morning, Minelva," Mummy said. She didn't wait for Minelva to answer but turned her back on the woman.

Mummy gazed down into the sink and saw nothing else but a dirty washrag that held a distinct trace of my monthlies. She rested her hands on her hips, tapping a foot on the wet, cement floor.

"When you get your period?" She stared at my crotch as if it would respond.

My eyes tingled. "It came for the first, yesterday."

"What did you use that rag for?" Mummy looked straight into my eyes.

"I fold it up and use it like a pad."

A stiff breeze crossed my face and left it stinging. My whole body erupted in uncontrollable shudders and I sobbed so hard that crying stifled my breath.

"Why?" Mummy waved me into the shower. "You're supposed to tell me when these things happen. I'm supposed to tell you what to do when these things happen. I'm supposed to show you how to put on a sanitary pad so you don't mess up your clothes. I was nine, three years younger than you, when I got mine and I went and told my mother. And my mother washed my whole skin and showed me what to do. You just come and want to deprive me of that?"

I kept quiet the whole time, partly because I felt humiliated. Mummy scrubbed me down like an impatient groomsman. Each stroke carried the weight of her words on my body. She reached between my legs and realized how rough she was when I flinched from her touch. Mummy took one look at me and when she saw the pain on my face, her angry expression dissipated into something that was softer and apologetic. Her touch became gentle.

"When you bathe, make sure you wash out yourself properly. If you don't wash between your legs carefully, you will smell. And this thing carries a high odour so do what I say and don't embarrass me. People don't like to smell this. They do nothing but smear you in public when you don't take care of these things. You understand?"

I nodded at her.

"Keep away from those wayward girls who do nothing else but talk about boys and the ungodly things they do behind their parents' backs. Their talk will sound sweet like a fairy tale but don't get fooled. In reality that kind of talk is nothing but a bunch of lies, pure filth and nastiness."

Mummy soaped up my skin. She stopped, pointed at me, then wet the rag to wash it clean. Her face was straight and her eyes no longer had the gentle look I was accustomed to seeing. They were intense looking and scary. "When you go and try all the things that they did and you get yourself in trouble, then they'll turn round and give you a bad name, laugh to your face and spread a ton of gossip about you."

"You have to stop playing with boys now." Her voice went deep and threatening. I wondered why? One of my friends had a sister two years older than me and she plays with us when she felt like. Having a period didn't stop her from playing.

"From today, all that liming, riding up and down the place like you're one of them, done. No more basketball, no marbles and that bike have to stay in the house from now on. Don't let me catch you at any time with none of them boys from round here. They will pick up the scent and once a man finds out that you get your monthlies, they come after you to love up. So mind yourself, you hear?"

She put me under the shower to rinse off. "We talk gone change from today. I want you to tell me everything so don't keep any more secrets from me." She turned off the pipe and wrapped a towel around me. "As a woman you must walk straight in order to go through life as a decent person. I want you to get a book and inside write down the day your period starts and the day it ends, and each month bring that book to me so I can keep track of it too. You don't go 'round talking about your period as if it was common conversation. So don't tell a soul. This is a private matter. Don't laugh up with any man or you'll get pregnant. When you don't see your period, come and let me know."

She patted her chest hard for emphasis, so I knew it was important for me to do as she said. "I'll take you straight to the doctor. Go to your room. I'll come and show you what else to do."

***

Daddy saw me snivelling when I hurtled past him toward my bedroom.

"What happen to Michelle?" I peeped through the crack in the door. His tone was uncertain. His eyes narrowed and his eyebrows were squished together.

Mummy's feet pattered toward my bedroom door. "She's seeing her period."

"Jesus Christ! What are you going to do?" He flinched and clutched his chest with his arms. There was this frightened look on his face. Mummy crossed her arms on seeing all this. I heard her suck her teeth at him.

"We're going to talk to her about these things."

"Full stop." He held his hands up as if he were being arrested. "You know I can't deal with them women's issues. This is your territory."

"This is your one and only child, mister man. You need to watch out for all those men who love to sniff at young women."

Daddy scratched his head as if he didn't know what to say or do about me. He walked over to the dining room table and leaned onto the back of one of the chairs, looking troubled, as if the world was crashing around him. "I don't deal good with them kinda things, Cora. Take her to my mother and save us the headache."

***

Mama looked stunning for a woman in her sixties. She had no grey hairs, but Mummy said Mama puts a warm brown colour in her hair because she felt she was still young. Mama always had somewhere to go and something to do and didn't allow age to stop her from living. She gave up karaoke just to have a talk with me that evening.

I loved my grandmother.

"I understand you didn't tell Cora when you started menstruating and that you went with a washrag between your legs. So already you're keeping secrets from your mother." She patted the long chair for me to sit next to her.

Mama's voice was gentle. She never raised it in anger and she didn't make you feel ashamed about anything. She smiled at me and I smiled back at her.

"I wasn't keeping it a secret." I'm not one of those girls who get on crazy and excited over having a period. I'm not ready to be a woman. I love my life the way it was two days ago. My head hurts. I have bad cramps. I felt nasty and I didn't know how to tell Mummy about it. We never had a conversation about any of this and I'm not sure if I want to have that kind of talk with her, either.

"But I know what menstruation is because it came to one of the girls in school and when everyone saw the red stain on the back of her uniform, they starting teasing her as if it were a joke."

"How did you feel?" Mama asked.

I didn't find it was funny at all. I felt embarrassed for her. The girl's parents got her transferred to another school because she was too shame to come back.

"Mummy overreacts over everything. All the time she never had a problem where I go and who I go with. I used to take up my bike and go all over with my friends. You know that, too, cause we will pass by for some water and something to eat. I used to go cross the road and shoot two hoops and pitch three marbles with them same boys too, and she never had a problem with that. But all of a sudden – this, that and the next and she's getting on fussy and saying I mustn't go nowhere. If that is the case this period better go back where it come from because I don't want no part of it."

Mama blinked her eyes and cocked her head to one side as if she were surprised at me for saying this.

"I'm not saying that you can't play with boys but, you can't expect to have your period and still gallivant up and down the place with them like you used to. Right now you're at that point in your life that you can get pregnant. You're not a little child anymore and you must be aware that there are consequences for your actions now."

Mama pressed her hand onto mine and gave it a soft squeeze. "You may be angry because your free paper burn but Cora is only trying to protect you. And I know she seems unreasonable and unfair but that is just love."

She winked at me, then smiled. "Michelle, I know you don't like to talk, but remember you can tell me anything. When you don't feel comfortable talking to Cora, come and see me." She put an arm around my shoulder. "You know how I flex."

I told Mama everything that happened this morning, and she laughed until tears sprang down her face.

"That's the reason why you decide to take it upon yourself to walk round with the rag between your legs?"

Mama's laugh was like the sound of someone trying to start a stalling vehicle. She held her stomach and bent over in front of me, unable to control herself. Goosebumps covered my arms, but after thinking about it I started giggling. It really was silly of me.

Mama coughed to clear her throat, and then wiped her tears in the sleeves of her blouse.

"Let me tell you something. This is nothing to be ashamed of. I went through it and so did your mother. We women have to go through life with pain and suffering all the time. This is just another road that you must cross in becoming a woman. You're lucky you didn't born in my day when I had to wear a piece of cardboard between my legs and tie it down with a belt around my waist."

My eyes widened and my mouth opened. *How uncomfortable*, I thought. Mama threw her head back again and chuckled at my expression. I didn't see what was funny about walking around with cardboard between your legs. It made me grateful for the sanitary pads at the supermarket. Mama nudged me in my sides with her elbow, which made me laugh along with her.

"Look, your mother is just scared. She will have to go through this alone too, because your father cut from the same cloth as he own father. They don't have the stomach to deal with things like these. If you look around the village, you'll see more than enough pregnant tweens to count on them fingers of yours. Cora doesn't want you to become one of them. She has high hopes for you. But, I don't agree with half the things she has told you. Would you like me to have a chat with her?"

I nodded.

Mama walked me home that night and had a long talk with my mother. Things weren't so weird and scary after that, and strangely enough, I didn't feel like playing with the boys anymore. Mummy treated me normal again in the months that passed. She even allowed me to ride my bicycle again, but only when she was at home.

The days that followed were quiet. The weeks that passed were still. I could never prepare my mind and body for her comings. My stomach cramped and I felt bloated and uncomfortable every time. Sometimes her visits were short and sometimes she overstayed.

I thought she was being unkind and I wish she didn't exist. But, there were signs of her coming long before my eyes had learned to see. I know now that my discomforts were her cues; that she did allow me to understand - to make the necessary arrangements.

It was me who failed to be hospitable.

My Legs Quivered
Lady B

My legs quivered; clitoris engorged and throbbing.

As I lay sprawled across the bed in the aftermath of a glorious orgasm, guilt engulfed me. This was wrong; I never intended to do this. After all I was only nine years old. How did I end up here?

Let's go back to the beginning of this day and the beginning of this path.

It was another ordinary day in my island paradise - the wind blowing gently as the rays of the sun danced among the many fruit trees on my immediate surroundings. I was doing what any nine-year-old girl was expected to be doing: outside playing. This was no "girly" playing though, no dolls, no tea parties, and no "cooking". I hated all of that feminine stuff.

In my mind, I was a powerful boy.

I rode my bike, whisked up and down my gap on roller skates, and climbed the mango tree in search of lunch after exhausting bouts of exertion.

I usually played alone because the other girls thought I was too rough - except this one girl. Her chiselled features and unsmiling face scared off potential friends. Therefore she was all mine. We played until our parents called us in for dinner.

When dinner was over I decided to go over to her house so we could continue enjoying each other's company. I ran with glee and excitement to the short distance to her house at the end of my gap.

I knocked at the door rapidly, eager to see her again. I waited for what seemed like an eternity. The door opened and I ran into the house. "Latoya! Latoya! You ready to go back outside and skate? Latoya!!"

I got no answer. How strange. Was she mad at me because I threatened to throw her over her mother's fence earlier that day? Why wasn't she answering me?

I finally looked up to see who had opened the door for me. I had assumed it was Latoya's mother, but I was staring into the face of a complete stranger. I was frozen with mortification. I just ran past a complete stranger and started screaming for my friend. How rude! My mother would be horrified!

"Hey, I am Latoya's cousin from St. Vincent," she said in a singsong accent. The words were strung together like a calypso song and I was simply fascinated. What a gorgeous foreign creature!

She had dark chocolate skin like me but she was tall and possessed facial features that reminded me of people I saw on television. She looked exotic and her accent thrilled me. She started to tell me her name and introduced herself but I was so caught up in her mesmerizing way of speech, I did not hear a word.

"You can have a seat and wait for Toya, she will be back soon."

I snapped out of my trance and sat down on my favourite couch in the living room. The foreign creature began to lock the door and close the windows as I sat twiddling my fingers with impatience, wondering how long Latoya would take to return home.

She went upstairs and left me alone downstairs. After

about five minutes of humming to myself, she invited me upstairs to watch some movies in her room while I waited. I ran up the stairs in eager anticipation of dissipating my utter boredom. I typically couldn't keep still for more than ten minutes.

She beckoned me to her bed and told me to sit while she found a movie. As I sat and she reached over me to grab her videotapes, her breasts were rubbing against my thighs. It gave me the weirdest sensation and I felt guilty for even entertaining the thoughts. After all, this was an innocent touch.

She retrieved the tape she was looking for and asked me to put it into the VCR. When I came back to the bed, she started asking me about my hobbies while playfully twirling my hair-twists in her fingers. The playful twirling turned into a head massage, and then a shoulder massage and soon she had worked her way down to my back.

I became relaxed, languid and comfortable. Foreign creature was cool. I was beginning to like her, thinking that maybe we could hang out like me and Latoya usually did. In the midst of my musing, I felt her massaging hands kneading my buttocks. It sent strange sensations through my body, leaving me craving something unknown.

I felt guilty.

Here I was turning an innocent massage into something sexual and nasty. I banished my thoughts and let her continue.

"Turn over so I can massage the front now. This will relax you more."

"Ok...but isn't that a little strange?"

"No, professional masseuses do it like this. Guess you have never heard of a full body massage," she said.

"No, I never have."

"Just turn over," she said in a soothing tone.

"Are you supposed to massage my breasts like that?"

"Yes, this is all part of the massage, just relax, I know what I am doing."

"Ok...but are you sure you are supposed to be massaging my nack nack?"

"Yes, this is a part of a massage. You need to get exposed to more cultures and experiences."

I tried to put my mind in a place of relaxation instead of feeling dirty as she squeezed my nipples and rubbed the lips of my "nack nack". But my "nack nack" kept getting wetter and wetter as she massaged it while simultaneously squeezing my nipples.

It felt good, too good, and wrong. My mother always told me to never let boys touch my "nack nack" but she never said anything about girls. I convinced myself that I wasn't doing anything wrong.

In the midst of grappling with my inner feelings, I felt her hot, wet tongue lapping at the bud in my "nack nack". The bud started to throb and pulse as extremely pleasurable sensations coursed through my body.

What was she doing? Is this all part of the massage too?

As her mouth closed in on the bud and she began sucking, I began to feel a build up of pressure.

It felt so good I could cry.

I knew from watching my parents' porn collection that this must be what they refer to as "cumming". The pleasurable feeling increased in intensity, my breathing quickened, my bud hardened and I felt liquid spouting down there as I instinctively screamed "I'm cumming! I'm cumming!"

She looked up at me and smiled with liquid dripping from her lips.

"I'm sorry I peed on you. I am so embarrassed. I-I-I thh…ii…nn…kkk I should go home now."

"Noo don't go, you didn't pee yourself. That was just your female cum."

"Female what?"

"It is the liquid that comes out after you orgasm. Men have a white sticky cum but the female one can feel like peeing."

"I still think I should go home" I said, while looking at the floor in shame, contemplating what I had just done.

"Didn't it feel good?"

"Y…y…y…ee…sss" I stuttered.

"Then come let me make you feel good again. Take off your clothes."

"Buuuuttt" I stuttered again.

"Take them off."

I complied, taking off my flowery vest and short pants which were now twisted onto a side. I stood before her naked. She stripped, revealing a pair of fully formed gorgeous breasts with pert nipples, a flat stomach revealing the beginnings of abs and a small, neat-shaven "nack nack".

In awe, I stood drinking in the sight of her as she glided across the floor. My gorgeous foreigner. She started touching my bud, eliciting the sensations again. As I felt myself floating into that surreal plane of ecstasy, she ordered me to lie down. I complied. I waited to feel that exquisite tongue touch me once more.

With my eyes closed, waiting in anticipation, I felt

something hot and wet touching me in my most private parts. It didn't feel like a tongue this time. I opened my eyes to see her spread-eagled across the bed, with her head resting on the foot of the bed while mine was at the top. Her feet were entangled with mine, forming the perfect shape of a scissors. Her throbbing bud brushed mine, ever so gently at first, but soon with more vigour and pace. Her pace became frantic. Her breath came in short spurts, and her juices flowed into mine.

A crescendo was building. Her bud got harder and rubbed against mine with more force. My bud also hardened and my privates became flooded. Liquid trickled from my privates to hers. The sound and scent were my aphrodisiac.

Indescribable pleasure coursed through my veins as we screamed out in unison. I felt a gush of liquid - not just from me this time, but also from her.

My legs quivered, my clitoris was engorged and throbbing. As I lay sprawled across the bed in the aftermath of a glorious orgasm, the guilt began to engulf me. This was wrong; I never intended to do this.

After all I was only nine years old.

COMING OUT

It's All Right
Kyrie

I was eighteen when I knew for certain that I loved women.

Before then, my appreciation for all the wondrous, intoxicating, powerful things women could do and be and hold - was largely theoretical.

I grew up a solitary, internal child, devoted to worlds of books; inventive hours spent scribbling at a desk, playful tea parties for imaginary friends, curated by my mother and attended by all the fantastical guests my imagination could conjure up.

If you're shaking your head in mild concern over whether I was strange, I'll be the first to proudly declare it: I was strange and I was lucky enough to be born into a household where strangeness was no sin.

This didn't mean that I had an unstintingly liberal upbringing - far from it. Despite being couched in many traditional mores, my parents, and principally my mother, always allowed me freedoms I was painstakingly aware other little girls and boys didn't enjoy. I read what I wanted, watched what I felt compelled to watch, and was given the gift of being able to admire humanity across the widest spectrum imaginable.

All of humanity.

So it was little wonder that I grew up with a vast, voluptuous appreciation for the female form. Breasts excited me. The lush, taut strength of women's thighs, flexed for dance; the resilient symmetry of a pair of bare calves tensed while a woman stood on tiptoe hanging laundry, reaching for a book, a dish or a set of crisply folded sheets. These things and so many others became part of my frequently-observed religion of visual delights.

My interest spanned far past the orbit of the physical. As I grew into my teenage years, conversations with women, especially those older and more world-versed than I, were interludes I sought out eagerly, preferring them to the graceless fumblings of male hands in sticky vinyl-upholstered backseats. Listening, rapt, to smart, sophisticated women, with silver-framed glasses and well-modulated foreign accents, expounding on their travels, cataloguing their adventures in academia or domestic wars - this was more exciting even than reading!

Here were living, breathing examples of everyday heroines, fiercely independent beauties helming their own fates without the yoke of menfolk reining them in.

It wasn't just elite-educated, fancily-attired women who fascinated me either. I grew up loving the calluses on farmgirls' palms; the gorgeous tattoo of Creole English punctuated with raucous laughter. I loved the sounds of shrewd barwomen upbraiding sour, crusty village drunks. I thrilled to the sights of Trinidad countrywomen setting *maticoor*[1] nights ablaze with wide-hipped, brown-limbed gyrating. Watching them dancing, kicking off their gold and silver strappy high heels to pound their bare soles into the earth, their heads thrown back exultantly, lines of clean sweat dripping from their chins and beading atop their crimson-painted lips, I felt an answering fire in the pit of my belly. Never did I dance as they danced. I did

---

[1] The Friday night of a Hindu wedding celebration, characterized by a female street procession, drumming, singing and dancing.

what I have always done - I waited, and watched, and wrote secret hungers in my journals. And I hoped that all I felt didn't just exist in the realms of theoretical fantasy. I, who adored literature in so many of its incarnations, who preferred living between pages profusely blessed with ink, did not want this truth about myself to be a fiction, a fanciful invention of an over-thinking girl's feverish mind.

I was eighteen when I had my first woman, and I was eighteen when I told this truth to my mother.

It's important to know that though I'd just turned eighteen; I did not think of myself as a "woman", not in the fullness, richness and depth I felt that word merited. Just as true as this was the fact the person I'd fallen in love with was definitely a woman herself. There were less than ten years between us, but those years were filled with travels and properly-adult decisions and sexual conquests on her end; things I hadn't begun to fathom doing myself. I spent much of my time with her marvelling that I, a bookish but gauche girl just on the verge of graduating secondary school could have so captured her interest - but oh, I believed every word she said. Even the way she looked at me told me in no uncertain terms, *"You are adored. Feel how much you are wanted by me. Feel how desperately, how achingly, I want you to be mine."*

I don't think I wanted anything more at the time than to be able to walk on the Promenade[2] holding her hand. Or to sit up on San Fernando Hill, eating coffee ice cream and kissing her neck, inhaling the goodness of her, delighting in her nearness without needing to dart behind a rock (or a public restroom, or a mercifully-positioned tree trunk in the Botanical Gardens). I knew from early

---

[2] Brian Lara Promenade, Port of Spain, Trinidad.

on that in Trinidad, the way we loved necessitated subterfuge. I got good at hiding her, not because I wanted to, but because I knew what would happen. I didn't have to imagine too hard to conjure up thoughts of angry phone calls to my house, of raised voices hurling choice cuss words across telephone lines, of the stinging disappointment that would linger in eyes and gestures. Of her face streaked with tears, voice cracked open with pain and the terror of a future in which we would be allowed to be together and allowed to be proudly Trini - but not both. Not on this soil. I learned, as queer women who inhabit Caribbean space do, how to give up.

I couldn't give up telling my mother.

It was a few days before Christmas and we'd gone to her friend's house for a party. I remember the shoes I wore and the skirt; I remember dressing up, selecting makeup I was unaccustomed to using. Carefully lining my lips felt, ridiculously, like going in to battle. I didn't know how I would tell her. Words had been my business all my life, and she above all others, was the reason I honoured writing. But I felt certain that my words would fail me then - that I would blurt out the confession. I imagined it dangling in the stifled air between us, bare and gleaming, demanding a response she wouldn't be able to give.

We sat close together while the parang[3] band burst into their *serenal*[4], setting the quiet night to dancing. Tables and chairs were pushed back beneath the tented clearing behind my mum's friend's house and men and

---

[3] Seasonal folk music of Trinidad and Tobago, of Venezuelan provenance, typically played around Christmas time and traditionally sung in Spanish.
[4] A song in which parang players announce their arrival and tell the story of Christ's birth.

women began to sway and dingolay in earnest. Fingers clicked in perfect sync to the rhythms of an artfully-strummed cuatro, of a hearty basso profundo and a lilting second soprano crooning lyrics devoted to the Christ child, to the joy and mirth associated with his birth. I stole a glance at my mother's face. She was beaming, the reflected glow of red and green fairy lights giving her features a charming, whimsical tint. She looked so happy in that moment. I realized, with a clarity that nearly made me gasp aloud, that though I might love my girlfriend with more in me than I knew I had - though I might yet love scores of women in the life still left me - there would be no woman's face I loved seeing more than my mother's.

"Mummy," I blurted. My palms were slick with sweat, leaving damp patches when I pressed them onto my skirt. My mother's feet were tapping to the music, and when she turned to watch me, an irrepressible grin lingered around her mouth, bunching her cheeks with childlike merriment.

"I love Radha," I said, feeling the words surge out of me, as ungainly and awkward as I knew they would be. No elaborate framing of my years of Sapphic inclinations coming to bear fruit, no reasonable preface for the formation of these new and blistering desires. Just my voice, trembling and quiet beneath the full song of worshipful reverence, belted out by the band. Just my voice, offering three damning, shy words.

I love Radha.

"Kyrie," my mother said, a kind frown knitting between her eyebrows, her feet stilling in the middle of their parang patterns. "I know that, honey."

I felt myself shaking my head, with all the

desperation of a small child who resorts to jerking, panicked body motions when it feels certain that words aren't working. I couldn't make my words work. I could barely summon them to rise forth from my chest.

"No," I helplessly whispered. "No, Ma. Not...not like that. Yes, like that, but."

Vaguely, as if through a waterfall of echoing chac-chacs, I heard my mother say my name again. In her mouth, my name was a question, a wondering, and in her voice I heard the very first beginnings of her world - the world in which I was an understood set of things - begin to shift. I was responsible for that tilt, and I didn't know what it would mean. But I knew I couldn't take it back. Doggedly, I worked to pry loose the only other words I could say, staring into her eyes.

"I mean. I mean she's more than my friend. I mean I... I love her. I love her and it's not going to go away, Ma. It's not."

In the moments that ticked between us after I shut my mouth, there wasn't any silence. The parang band had swung their set into overdrive, their claves knocking out a rich, wooden tattoo, their guitars held in masterful embraces, promising skirt-whirling melodies for hours to come. It wasn't the theme music I would have picked for my big reveal, but it was the music I got and it was more glorious than anything I myself could have composed.

I was eighteen and so scared.

My mother nodded, once, slowly. She didn't reach across to clasp my sweaty hand in hers; she didn't clap me on the back with false congratulatory zeal. She nodded.

"Alright," she said.

I still can't say for sure whether she meant it or not. Maybe she used the word "alright" as a placeholder, the way people do when there truly are no words to be said. *Alright. Okay. Yeah.* Maybe when she said it then, she thought, "Lord, it will never be alright again."

She knew, like I did, that it was one thing to have brought me up in frank admiration of women and another to be partnered to a woman in Trinilandia, where we gyrate near-nude, glitter-plastered, for two sun-scorched days of bacchanal-flavoured excess, then spend much of the rest of the year denying that we've even got private parts.

My mother wasn't born a queer ally. She became one through loving me.

Now I'm approaching my thirties and I no longer live in my mother's house, though I visit her often and I speak to her every day. In the near ten years that have passed since I came out to her, a great deal has changed, and some things have stayed the same. I'm not with Radha any longer, and I still love women. I'm in love with a woman right now, and I have this feeling...this persistent, bedrock-deep, firmament-vaulted feeling, that I will love her forever. I know that I can talk about her with my mother from now until the end of time.

We might not delve into details, like the way my lover's hair glows in the sunlight, or the particular sadness in her polite smiles, or the rhythm of her voice on the telephone, how it lists with weary adoration when we've stayed up all night talking into the morning, how we never want to say goodbye. How, in the most ineffable of ways, we never really do. How my lover knows things about me that I'll never tell another soul, because some things can only be said once, then sealed with tears, liquor and wordless vows.

My mother and I will never talk about my lover in

ways that I know are too sharp, too nude, too close to the marrow to handle. You know what, though? That's all fine. It is, as she put it a decade or so ago, in the middle of a festive Christmas evening, "alright." Even if that wasn't true then, it's true now, and I can talk to my mother about what matters most.

"Is there love there, Kyrie? Are you loved by Her, honoured, respected? Is your love safe, with Her?"

"Oh, Mummy. Yeah. I am. I am, by Her, and then some. There's love there. There is love, and I'm safe."

Where is the love?
wänd(HER)lust

"As I think about anyone or anything - whether history or literature or my father or political organizations or a poem or a film - as I seek to evaluate the potentiality, the life-supportive commitment/possibilities of anyone or any thing, the decisive question is, always, *where is the love?*"[5]
~ June Jordan

"Where is the Love?" Depending on your generation, the pivotal question could send you head-bopping to the beats of the American hip-hop group, the Black Eyed Peas, or gently mouthing along to the mellow sounds of Roberta Flack and Donny Hathaway. For me, a Black Pan-African feminist raised between the harmattan heat of the West African coast and the periwinkle shores of the Caribbean sea, this question is so poignant and reminiscent of the spirit and words of Caribbean-American writer and activist June Jordan. For it was in a packed auditorium at Howard University in 1978, that June Jordan chose to lay herself bare by defining her feminism, her Blackness, her "Self" as intrinsically connected as she posed the question: *"Where is the Love?"* It was also in that moment that she sought to critically define her understanding of Black feminism as a crucial

---

[5] Jordan, June. *Poetry for the People: A Revolutionary Blueprint.* Taylor & Francis. 1995.

act of love.

Black girl family values

Loving women was just not something we did in my family. In my family women went to school, studied hard, graduated from university, got a "good" job, married men and I guess, lived happily ever after? But that was the problem - deep in my Black girl heart I knew that wasn't going to be me. That wasn't going to be my future - not all of it anyway. I did study, I did work hard, and I did graduate. I did get a job and my family was proud. I let them bask in the glory.

I remember sitting through Sunday evening dinners - fried plantain, rice and peas and a side of gay bashing. "I just don't get why those gays have to hold hands in public anyway," they'd say. "Why must *they* dress like that?" "I don't mind the women you know (well that was a relief!). It's the men I just don't get"... (sigh!)

...and so the diatribes would continue and so my heart would hurt.

I remember how I'd squirm in my seat avoiding questions about why I never brought men home as I'd sit there picking at the chicken bones on my plate, which might as well have been my own - cold, bare and chewed up.

It was in those moments that I'd look up towards the stars and think of June Jordan in that crowded Washington D.C. auditorium and I'd whisper softly to myself in between the tears: Where is the Love? Where is the *fucking* love?

Love is in the People

I think back to all the women whom I have loved

and there have been many - my mother, my art history teacher at university, and my yoga instructor. I have loved women as sisters and as friends; I have loved women as colleagues and as mentors; I have loved women as partners and as momentary lovers. I have loved women physically and I have loved them emotionally. I have loved women in dreams and in living colour. I have loved in hotel rooms, in train stations, across cyberspace, in kitchens, in classrooms and in dancehalls. In all of these spaces and places women have rocked me to the depths of my core.

I remember the first time I loved a woman…and I mean really admitted to myself that I was in love with someone whom I knew I wasn't allowed to love (in that way) and I remember doing it anyway. I also remember the second and the third and I remember the last.

I remember the first time that I kissed a girl that I thought I loved - I was ten years old. Like Nel and Sula, Toycie and Beka Lamb, Gwen and Annie John,[6] we were inseparable. We walked home from school together, we'd do our homework together, go to the movies together, we'd do everything - together. We would also kiss each other every week after school pretending it was "nothing" but at the same time knowing it was something we weren't *allowed* to do. I looked forward to our after school kisses - her lips were smooth and I remember the way she took to my mouth like a playground, swinging and sliding around with the softness of that Black girl tongue. I loved that she made possible (and normal) my own curious

---

[6] *Sula* is a 1973 novel by Nobel Prize-winning author Toni Morrison, *Beka Lamb* is the debut novel from Belizean writer Zee Edgell, published in 1982; and *Annie John* is a novel written by Antiguan author Jamaica Kincaid in 1985. All three novels outline friendships between the characters mentioned.

desires.

I remember the first time a woman made me cum. I knew right then that I was in love - Oh, was I in love with that Black girl tongue! I was seventeen and not fully prepared for the fire that she would set alight in my belly. I remember how like a beautiful brown soucouyant[7] she would kiss my throbbing lips and set my skin on fire. I would pray for rain, freedom rain - the gushing kind that eventually came. All along I knew we were doing things we weren't *supposed* to do, but I would fall in love with her resistance - "fuck the world" she'd say. "It's only you and me here." I loved that I felt loved in the tightness of her orgasmic embrace.

I remember the first time a woman broke my heart. We were in university and had loved each other all semester until she decided she would get married to a man because it was something her family wanted her to do... it was something African girls were *supposed* to do. I remember how I cried and how my heart hurt and how I resigned myself never to love another woman again. I was so done with that Black girl tongue! How could I have loved her anyway? Black girls didn't love each other - not like that anyway... It wasn't something we were *supposed* to do.

I remember how I started loving men instead. I kissed them and fucked them and let them penetrate my body, dagger my soul, and duttywine my backside... but it was my heart, my heart, my heart that yearned for more of the tenderness of that Black girl love. How I yearned

---

[7] Soucouyants belong to a class of spirits called jumbees. Some believe that soucouyants were brought to the Caribbean from European countries in the form of French vampire-myths. These beliefs intermingled with those of enslaved Africans.

for the tenderness of that Black girl tongue that would stroke my heart and gently caress my soul. I remember that love was in the beautiful woman that found me hurting and that brought me back to myself. Love was in the woman that loved me through words; the woman talked to me in tongues sharing Music, Malcolm X, Magic and Me. Love was in the gentleness and tightness of her embrace. Love was in the seriousness of her voice as we read to each other Pat's poetry:

"Sister, love

I carry you with me, talk with you, ask your opinion

you cannot give me up, I cannot give you up.

We are linked in our Blackness, our creativity, our queerness

our muses conspire.

I never promise to write often

to call often

to be a presence

I promise

to love you and call you

sister."[8]

Love was in those words and others (her own) that helped me find strength, and courage, and power… again. Love was in her reminder that sometimes the people that claim to love us the most also struggle to love the fullness and complexities of who we are; they fail to love all the bigness and beauty of who we are - and in those moments we have each other: brave Black girls who love and

---

[8] Parker, Pat. 'For Audre.' *Callaloo*. Vol. 23, No. 1, Gay, Lesbian, Bisexual, Transgender: Literature and Culture (Winter, 2000), pp. 68-72. Published by: The Johns Hopkins University Press.

protect each other. That, right there, is where the love exists.

Love is in the Politics

I still struggled to reconcile my family's abhorrence for the woman I was and the women I had loved. I didn't tell them. I loved them too much. I loved me too much.

It really surprised me though. After all, it was from these women that I learned to live this thing I had come to call "feminism." It was from them that I had learned to love and be loved, it was from them that I had learned to hold and be held, it was from them I observed womanist bravery, power, hard work, and self-worth. Yet in spite of all the things I learned from the women who raised me, it was from these same women that I also learned to loathe everything about who I was - a Black girl who loved other Black girls (in ways she wasn't *allowed* to).

I came to terms with the fact that they might never embrace the fullness of who I was and how I'd chosen to love, but that I would be ok. I would find love in a carefully crafted "intentional" and "political" family.

I would find love in the politics and pages of Black feminist/womanist writing. I would find love in the arms and words of feminist mothers and aunties and friends that would hold me, nurture me and love me. It was in my exploration of Audre's words, Toni's stories, Patricia's pedagogy that I learned to love my Black girl self and re-learned my love for that Black girl tongue. It was in those pages and in those words that I came to see myself and my Black girl love as a powerful means of resistance in the cold concreteness of the harsh jungle I had found myself navigating.

In Patricia Hill-Collins' seminal text *Black Feminist*

Thought: Knowledge, Consciousness, and the Politics of Empowerment she talked about Black womanhood and the need to broaden the spectrum of Black women's relationships as means of reclaiming the power of deep love.[9] It was in this critical text that she taught me how loving relationships between Black women could come to constitute a form of resistance. It was in her words that I came to see the myriad of transformative possibilities imbued by my own Black girl love.

In her groundbreaking essay, "Uses of the Erotic: The Erotic as Power," Audre Lorde explores the fundamental link between deep feelings and power. In it she says:

"There are many kinds of power, used and unused, acknowledged or otherwise. The erotic is a resource within each of us that lies in a deeply female and spiritual plane, firmly rooted in the power of our unexpressed or unrecognized feeling. In order to perpetuate itself, every oppression must corrupt or distort those various sources of power within the culture of the oppressed that can provide energy for change. For women, this has meant a suppression of the erotic as a considered source of power and information in our lives."[10]

It was in my reading of Audre's definition of the erotic that I came to see my sexuality, my queerness, my Black girl love as a reflection of my power in a world where Black girls are made to believe they have none. Audre's words, Pat's poetry, Patricia's pedagogy offered a salient moment of self-reflection for this Black girl. It was

---

[9] Hill Collins, Patricia. *Black Feminist Thought: Knowledge, Consciousness, and the Politics of Empowerment.* Boston: Unwin Hyman, 1990.
[10] Lorde, Audre. *Sister Outsider.* Berkeley: Crossing Press. p. 53. (1984).

in their words that I discovered the revolutionary power of my own Black girl love. It was in the poetics, and prose and power of Black feminist pedagogy that I found the love.

Love We Ah Practice
"We have to consciously study how to be tender with each other until it becomes a habit because what was native has been stolen from us, the love of Black women for each other. But we can practice being gentle with each other by being gentle with that piece of ourselves that is hardest to hold, by giving more to the brave, bruised girlchild within each of us." ~ **Audre Lorde**

    I often think about what I would say to June Jordan if I was sitting in that auditorium in Washington D.C. that day in 1987. What could I possibly say? As I think about this straightforward yet powerful question, *"Where is the love?"* I reflect again on Audre's words: "we have to consciously study how to be tender with each other until it becomes a habit". I imagined Audre calling for a love beyond words - a lived, practiced, political love.
    I thought about my own life and my own experiences. I think of *where* I have found love and *how* I have found love. I would tell June how I discovered love in the hands and hearts of women that I allowed to hold me and who allowed me to hold them back. I would tell her how contrary to what we were *"allowed"* to do, we Black girls were (and are) transgressive - we etch signs of love on our skins with our Black girl tongues on a daily basis. I would tell her that I found love, and power and other strategies of resistance in her words and the words of other feminist women that have taught me the

revolutionary power of love. I would tell her that love is in our hearts, each of us, but that we must be brave and intentional about finding it and sustaining it. I would tell her that as we Black girls discover the dangerous and wicked ways of a world that consistently tells us that we can't, that we aren't enough, that we don't exist, it is imperative that we love each other fiercely…that we simply do not give up.

And as I sit here in this overcrowded bus looking out of the window, sweat rolling down my forehead in the stillness of this Caribbean summer time heat - I think of June, Audre, Pat, Patricia, my mother, my first, my second, my third and my last Black girl loves, the ones that loved me and let me love them back and I hear the words of reggae artist Tanya Stephens reverberating through the speakers: *"we ah go stand firm put up a Black fist and mek dem know seh ah love we ah practice…Lace up yuh boots and prepare for the revolution."* [11]

And that's what I'd tell June:

Love is in the people.

Love is in the politics.

Love is in the practice.

---

[11] Stephens, Tanya. *Nah Run* Hold on Riddim. (2008).

My Sexuality and My Church
Anonymous

"Sinner."

"Hell bound."

"Abomination."

"Abnormal."

These were some of the words I grew up hearing as a child - phrases and words that were used by preachers from my church to describe people who were homosexual. At thirteen years old, I remember feeling warm with fear as I crushed on my Sunday School teacher. It was something about the way she spoke, the way she looked, her ability to calm a room of frisky teens with her soothing voice. My world stood still when she smiled at me and my palms got sweaty every time she called me to read a memory verse or explain the Holy Spirit to the class.

By the time I turned fourteen I was incapable of keeping my feelings to myself, so I told her how I felt. Flash forward one day later: I am sitting in my Pastor's office with my mother, Sunday School teacher and a deliverance minister. I knew what was about to happen. Cue the prayers, blessed oil, confession sessions and tears from my mother. It was honestly the worst feeling in the world. I was later forced to endure deliverance services repetitively for four hours a day, two days a week for the next two months. I knew having sexual feelings for a woman was wrong and I wanted to be free. I wanted to be cured from my gayness so that I wouldn't go to hell. I wanted to be loved by Jesus and I knew (based on teachings) that he wouldn't love me if I were a nasty, dirty, lesbian.

"Yes, thank you Jesus. I am free! I am Free!" I shouted at the end of three weeks. I had no choice really. I was tired and I didn't feel any love from the people who claimed to love me. I needed to escape.

For the next four years I sank into depression. I had no friends at school, few at church and a reputation that was not pleasing to family or God. I constantly told my mother I was healed and that God had cured my gayness, but that was a lie. Internally, I wrestled with the feelings and began to hate God because he had not fixed me. To relieve my sexual frustration I binge-watched lesbian porn and fantasized about having a wife in a world where that was acceptable. In my lesbian world, women were happy and it was okay to live as you felt.

Eventually I was able to distinguish between what I knew and how I felt. This distinction confused me more: "If I have to like guys, why am I not attracted to them? Why do I find the mere thought of women sexually enticing? What the fuck is wrong with me! Oh fuck, I'm starting to curse now. Another sin to go to hell for..."

Sunday after Sunday in church began to choke me. I was dying and no one around me seemed to notice. I couldn't take it anymore; maybe suicide was a good option. I soon found a release: I began slicing the palm of my hands as I listened to music that spoke about running away and escaping the hells of this world. The blood and pain removed the pain I felt internally, if only for a minute. It was not ideal for any human being to feel alone, lost and confused in life. I felt like that every second.

To prove my "straightness", I forcefully changed my "tomboy look" to a more feminine one. I then did the grossest thing imaginable to me and found myself a gullible young man who I called "boyfriend". I was promoted to the youth leader position at church and was actively involved in Ministry. Mom was happy and my Pastor was greatly pleased because it reinforced that gay people can be fixed. Externally, I behaved the way I was expected to behave.

Then I met Julie...

At eighteen years old, I was now a student at University. I remember heading to class when she stopped me and urged me to fill out a questionnaire. Julie promised it would only take ten minutes. Two hours later we were still engrossed in deep conversation as my classmates came looking for me, enquiring why, for the first time in life, I missed an English class (who misses English?!). Julie, however, became my study.

Effortlessly, that conversation evolved to three-hour phone conversations and random "dates". Neither of us came clean of our intentions and it was that mystery that kept us both intrigued. My silence was strictly based upon the fact that she was a PK (Pastor's kid), and six years my senior. I was not going to jeopardise my presumed straightness for a crush.

The silence soon ended. We both agreed to meet up in the city a Sunday afternoon after our respective church services were finished. Unable to decide what to do, I suggested we head to my home to watch a movie. My mom was out of the country and we were used to being alone together so I didn't expect anything spectacular to happen to me. When we arrived, however, Julie kept looking at me intensely. I had to ask if something was wrong. Instead of a verbal response she leaned towards me and gently kissed my lips. Noting my responsiveness, she slid her hands up my dress and began to explore every part of my body. An hour later all bases were covered and we were no longer "just friends".

"Are we together?" I'd ask her after sex.

"I'm not a lesbian," she would reply. "Plus this isn't really sex."

For the next two years this thing continued between us but after a while it felt as if we were slapping God in his face. I'd attend several of her family's prayer meetings at home. Her father, the Pastor, and his wife were very receptive to me; another young person vibrant for the Lord. During the prayer meetings however, Julie and I would sneak off to steal a kiss or more while her father was telling the devil he had no hold over our lives. I also learnt how to "sext" and a few minutes into the sermon on a Sunday morning, I was "wet" in church due to Julie's wild imagination.

My mother often tried to see what was going on and demanded I stop disrespecting God by using my cell in church; I stopped sitting near her. On the few occasions Julie and I were ever in the same church service, I would try so hard to avoid eye contact. Knowing that was my plan, she would message me to meet her in the washroom. I always did and that usually resulted in Julie pulling my tongue out of my head as I rubbed her clit while the congregation sang, "Our God is lifted up with a shout of joy!"

This relationship was not healthy anymore.

After weeks of deliberation on the next step, we finally agreed to pray together and cry out to God for help. Unknowing to me, my mother confided in Julie about my past homosexual behaviour and asked her to help me get through and over it, and this helped Julie stay strong. Instead of having sex, we would spend time talking about God and his word and if the desires came we would end the conversation and suffer in solitude. I continued to be a youth leader in church and Julie started Bible school and was being trained to become a pastor like her father. She then got a boyfriend to ease the whispers from among church folk about how close she and I were. I stayed single because I could not imagine sharing my life with anyone but her. We managed to stay "holy" for about two months but the sexual tension between us had peaked; and one Sunday after attending the same church service we returned to my home for lunch, which eventually led to us having sex with each other.

"Maybe we should end this. Stop talking to each other," Julie blurted out as she leaned over me to get her bra. "I'm preaching in church next Sunday. I don't want to upset God."

End this now? After all the sacrifices we both have been making for this to work? All the frustration! All the lies! And you want to end this now?!

"I love you Julie. I think I am in love with you."

"But I keep telling you hun, I am not gay!"

There I sat in my Pastor's office again. This time seemed worse. I was soon informed that Julie claimed to have a word from God soon after her sermon and was led to confess her sins; in the process she accused me of making uncontrollable sexual advances towards her. Of course, she was not gay, and never displayed those tendencies, so it was a very believable case against me.

"We have tried, but you are bent on sinning," Pastor approached me very aggressively. "I cannot have this spirit passing down to the congregation. You can no longer Minister at this church. Too many spiritual lives are at stake."

I remember feeling bitter, upset, angry, hurt, hateful...

"And you are to no longer try to contact Julie. Her parents are very upset about this. She is very traumatised by this. They let you in their home and you let the devil control your emotions."

I should have told him the truth but it made no sense. Julie had tainted my reputation, and with a history like mine, I realised the end.

"I will continue to pray that God has mercy on your soul...but people like you cannot enter the Kingdom of God." And with a look of disgust, I was asked to exit his office.

My journey home was filled with images of angels singing a furnace anthem as they threw a tar-like substance on me. Thoughts of my mother tossing my clothes out the house were next. I imagined her crying as she denounced motherhood, screaming to the world that she hated her lesbian daughter, who apparently forced a woman to have sex with her.

Reality stepped in as I turned my key into the door.

"Is it true?" she asked in a weary voice. She was sitting in the chair holding her towel. Her eyes were bloodshot red. I knew she had been crying.

"Most of it."

"Will you ever change?"

"I don't know."

"Why are you still standing at the door? Come inside girl." Her position was unchanged for the rest of the evening.

Soon enough the Pastor's family knew every detail of the situation, and within a few weeks the entire church knew. I bravely returned to church Sunday after Sunday to be greeted by whispers, avoidance and sermons about homosexuals, abomination and hell. The people I once spoke to frowned upon me and walked away if I attempted to greet them; the hugs I once received from deaconesses turned to quick, dry waves from afar; the laughs after church with fellow youth leaders were exchanged for grunts and stares. The love of the church was gone and I eventually stopped going to church.

The silence and lack of support forced me to resort to old habits: thoughts of suicide resurfaced, along with the arm cutting, depressing music, nightmares, hatred for God and the total disregard for human company. After months of zombie living, my mother came to me one evening and had a conversation that changed my life. Noting that she and I didn't speak beyond the formalities since that evening I came home, I was shocked she invited herself into my room. I knew she was observing my crumble, I knew it was hurting her, but I did not expect an ounce of understanding on her part.

"You are my child," she began. "I am not happy that you are not happy. I love you and will support you no matter what or who you are." As her eyes filled with tears, she managed to ask an important question. "Forget the church, forget people and their opinions, forget how I feel. Tell me, who are you?"

Who am I? I wasn't sure how to answer, but after

much thinking, I resorted to what I knew, the bible. "I am a chosen generation, a royal priesthood, a holy nation, a child of the King."

She smiled. "Okay great, so what do you want? Or rather, how do you want to live?"

"I do not know. There is a battle between what I know and how I feel."

"Has God ever failed? Has God ever judged or condemned you?"

"No."

"Then hold your head up high! God is on your side, he will make a way." Mom paused. "And I will always be here, supporting you, and no matter what you choose, I am proud to call you daughter."

The message from the church could have ruined my life if my mother was not there to support me. The church, as expected, never came around. I was shunned and disowned because of the selfish, prideful, ungodly nature of the members of my church.

I thank God for the strength he gave my mother, but what about those who have no mother? What about those voiceless youths who stand alone searching for someone to tell them they are loved? Will the church say, "Yes! Jesus loves you!" Or will the church say, "Fix your sin then come in the doors to Christ." Will we keep spreading hate or will we finally search the scriptures and live the life Christ demands? Will we encourage the broken to come to him? For what is the purpose of the church if not to be a shelter for the afflicted and a place of rest for the tormented spirit?

To paraphrase John Chapter 8:

"And the scribes and Pharisees brought unto him a woman taken in adultery; Now Moses in the law commanded us, that such should be stoned: but what sayest thou?"

"...he lifted up himself, and said unto them, He that is without sin among you, let him first cast a stone at her."

"And they which heard it, being convicted by their own conscience, went out one by one, beginning at the eldest, even unto the last: and Jesus was left alone, and the woman standing in the midst. When Jesus had lifted up himself, and saw none but the woman, he said unto her, Woman, where are those thine accusers? Hath no man condemned thee?"

"She said, No man, Lord. And Jesus said unto her, neither do I condemn thee: go, and sin no more."

LOVE AND INTIMACY

The Story of Us
Akelia Oliver

Contentment

Contentment was not just what I felt, but what I embodied as I drifted towards the parking area to meet a very interesting lady. Happiness was never what I aspired to - I imagined contentment to be a much more realistic and attainable state of being. Here I was; a young, black woman born and raised in the third world paradise of Trinidad and Tobago. Even though my intelligence was more through training than natural ability, my looks were not stereotypically pretty and I in no way, form or fashion, was privileged with generational wealth, had made *it;* despite the doubt and the anxiety.

Just a few hours prior I had received the call that revealed that I was now amongst the gainfully employed, which coincided serendipitously with my already standing plans of having a beer with my friend.

This knowledge, accompanied by the fact that this particular friend was a successful woman in her own right and that we were about to embark on an evening of film and drinks, completely free of the male presence, made me exude a confidence that was crafted and tested like the finest metals in the hands of a blacksmith.

Wrapped around me like a cloak, my confidence protected me from the judgemental gaze of others and allowed me to cast my own unto them. It was in engaging in this voyeuristic practice, that over the last few years of adult development, I realised the greatest burden of a woman was not the biblical shedding of blood, but the problematic romantic engagements with male counterparts.

Let me give prefix by disclosing that I am neither bitter nor scorned; most of my interactions with the other sex have been pleasant and mutually enjoyable. However I could not ignore the horror stories of my fellow women.

Stories of deep betrayals, emotional abuse that put black eyes to shame and the calculation lurking behind kind gestures and charm. While providing a listening ear, I also offered advice, both wanted and unwanted, believing myself to be amongst the lucky…the untouchables; that rare breed of woman that found contentment out of the arms of a man, that loved women instead of secretly competing with her sisters and that was so far removed from the heteronormative value system that she could envision floating above the pedestrian relation that was the male-female romantic interface.

Then, I saw him.

And now with hindsight offering a clarity that was missed in our exchange, I realised that like Alice, I too was about to fall deep into a hole and emerge into a new world that completely disregarded my concept of reality.

Him

I can remember it clearly, seeing him walking across my path, not even noticing me as I was almost completely shrouded between a construction and a stairway. Without thinking, I called out to him and when he turned, I was immediately transported into that girl years ago. He was that boy, simple but lovely, and I delighted in his ever-present joy while we exchanged pleasantries and inquisitions about each other.

He took my friend and I to her home and along the way invited us out for the following night. I consented, and to be honest, I was more pleased about the notion of having reliable transport for the occasion than actually spending time with him.

That Saturday night was to be my real celebration, my own little debutante's ball where I was to be introduced into society. It was just drinks with my circle in sparsely populated bars in the St. James area. However with self-narration, there is always a touch of grandiose in adjudicating the importance of one's activity.

So there we were, me lazily blowing smoke in his car while we waited to collect the first of the animated figures in my menagerie. She of course was late, almost ridiculously late as he himself was late to retrieve me. We waited downstairs while he poured us drinks and I laughed because I could not decipher if this was charming in his preparedness or a warning sign of impending alcoholism.

Regardless, as I sipped I considered him for the first time in years and realised that what was seen yesterday was more a projection than reality. He was not in fact the same boy, but he was now a man.

A man who appeared to have matured into a more complex person and at that time I started to appreciate that while he was still lovely, he was far from simple. Almost immediately my curiosity was piqued. I too was on a journey that led me further and further from the person that I was years ago, a far cry from the virgin; I was now closer to the whore, and proud of it. I touted my sexual liberty and politics at parties and social gatherings, in a way very much similar to a pastor from the pulpit.

At the conclusion of the night, considerably more than my curiosity was piqued. Fuelled by lust and inebriations, I accompanied him home to share conversation and a chaste night, with us sleeping on separate couches talking about everything and nothing until we were lulled into sleep. Breakfast was served and kisses shared sporadically with enough passion to ignite small fires in our wake, and as I floated off to my own home, I knew that there was no doubt that I was going to soon return.

This is how we continued, his home was my home, his embrace was my security and his compliments soothed like a warming salve to my soul.

I'll admit it - I was smitten.

Unfortunately, like every other beautiful day, the dark clouds soon followed and my bubble was about to burst. Much too soon, cracks began to appear in the wall of our budding relationship and feelings of frustration and disappointment emanated almost tangibly from us both. I couldn't grasp the dual dichotomy of a life he seemed to be leading - appearing sweet, intelligent and even loving in private and then devolving into an oblivious, inconsiderate simpleton when we inhabited public spaces.

Likewise he would lash out, never with words of course; that would have made my life much too easy. Subtleties were his main medium of communication, so I would have to observe and examine every gesture, every word choice, to gain some sliver of understanding to his real feelings, while he wore his glowing smile as a mask.

That smile that made me think of him as a beautiful sun God with mischievous eyes was now the main symbol of my resentment. So he would casually smile as he said the most hurtful things. Smiling as he told me that I was too "free".

Freedom

"I thought you loved my free spirit." I would plead with him and he would smile and say "I do, but not for *my* girlfriend". Matters weren't helped when my free spirit led me innocently into the bed of a new male friend.

To me there was no subterfuge; when one is away from home, one sleeps where one can. At least this was what I understood to be true.

I explained until I was hoarse in the voice that no embraces were shared; it was only peaceful slumber between people who had celebrated the libations with a fervent gusto. His reaction caused hours of internal debate, but never wavering, I concluded that in sleep, gender was not a factor.

I repeatedly tried to make him see that for me there was only him. Stupid girl I was, forgetting that I was no longer in my lady friend's home talking of film while enjoying beverages. I had fallen down the rabbit-hole and in this strange new world, the male ego was even more fragile, and while as an unattached woman I was admired for my intensity and liberal mind, as his plus-one I was shamed into a constant balancing act.

I was asking myself questions never before posed. Warning myself to not let my friendliness be mistaken for flirting, to be ever-present but not clingy, to be witty but never argumentative. In trying to understand him, I was losing sight of who I was, but yet I could not retreat, envisioning his trust and acceptance to be the ultimate prize.

So I battled on.

But like quicksand, the greater I struggled the faster I sank and soon I found myself at the bottom of a deep festering hole, hating him, hating myself, hating every kind word he gave to others. Jealousy and pettiness were now the coats I wore, while my cloak of confidence lay forgotten and tattered under the bed.

But in all of this turmoil, there was a port in the storm.

Sex

Sex was our port offering safe haven, common ground, the one place where it appeared that we had perfect communion; no moment of insecurity, no misinterpretation, just a synchronicity that was effortless yet deliberate.

In those moments when our bodies interlocked, magic happened. During the act, I would often exclaim, "I can't breathe" or "I can't think", which, funnily enough, are the sensations felt when one is drowning.

And drown I did.

Soaked in sweat, I would sink lower and lower until it felt like I was submerged in him, filled with him until consumption was the only accurate word that I could conjure in those times of cerebral inactivity. Just a few months before, I would have laughed at whoever predicted that I would have celebrated cerebral inactivity.

And celebrated was what I did, simply because in these instants, he was mine and while his macho pride would thump and wail that it was me who was in fact *his*,

I would secretly smile into his shoulder and think, "Yes I am yours but it is my body that grasps yours".

My old self would make fleeting appearances at this time, scrambling for any crumbs of control in the relationship. My friends would rage against him, blame him for stealing my heart and scream, "Off with his head!" However while it was flattering to be defended, it was unnecessary for I was not blind at this point.

He no longer was that person that wrote me sweet messages and there was no pretence between us. I knew and he knew. I just needed to accept, which is what happened the last time I saw him.

I returned to his bed to find that our harbour was destroyed, not even in this place was our solace shared. While my body responded to his skilful ministrations, the feeling of consumption was gone. In its place was the same doubt, worry and shame that often existed in most of our time together.

That's when I accepted it was over.

I danced with the sun God and while it was exciting and thrilling, the scars from the burns will be with me forever.

In perfect symmetry, we ended as we began - with him smiling at me while he drove me home, and as I vowed the first time that I would return, this time I vowed never again.

Organic Chemistry
Aletha Murray

I've been in love a few times, and in retrospect I know I've been in LUST a few times; sometimes I've been in both simultaneously. Learning that there is a difference, learning the difference, and recognising and exploiting that difference has made me more clear-eyed about emotion, myself and - grandiose as it may sound - destiny.

One of the first times I fell deeply in love I was a teenager, so my hormones were going berserk; at least compared to how they are now. Yet I wasn't really in lust with the person (let us call him Adam). I only know this now. It took a ridiculously potent physical attraction to another person (let's call him Zack), on whom I had a longstanding unrequited crush, to begin my personal journey of realising the difference between lust and love. I remember rationalising that as I had been in "love" with Zack first, jettisoning my long-term relationship with Adam, to fulfil my body's longing for Zack, was really the first love coming to the fore and manifesting my true destiny.

What bullshit.

I liked the guy, by all means; he was my first teenage crush, and I crushed for a long time, but what I was experiencing was amazing chemistry. Oh, our chemistry was potent, mind-numbingly, nerve-tingling potent. Zack eventually "gentle dumped" me, went back to the "friend zone" that he'd been in for years, and I patched it up with Adam. Zack's reasoning - or excuse - was that he wasn't good for me, and he knew he would eventually screw up our relationship. Besides, he really liked me as his best friend. We stayed best friends for about five years after that and eventually drifted apart amicably. That was lust number one on the journey of discernment.

The second time I fell in lust was with Tony when I was at university, in a long distance relationship with Adam, who I can truly say I was in love with. That long-term relationship from teenaged years through to my early twenties, shielded me as well as underprepared me for the minefield of sexually involved male-female relationships. I say this because my four-year relationship with Adam before I went to university, while not perfect, was damn near perfect. I thought then and am certain now that he loved me, for who I was on the inside. What bliss!

What I knew only cerebrally but not experientially, and was about to learn the hard way, was that sometimes, many times, men will say ANYTHING to get into your pants. I don't know if it makes me prudish to be proud that Tony got only halfway into my pants, but I'm still proud! Since I can't cheat; I'm logistically challenged when it comes to remembering which lies I told to whom; when I felt that crazed chemistry for Tony, I was convinced that I had to end my relationship with Adam - which I did - because I had found THE ONE. It was the only logical conclusion based on my attraction and my Tony-invaded thoughts, right?

I was wrong, but what an instructive mistake. The pain of Tony's ultimate rejection; the realisation that it was all just part of "the game" for him; the recognition of the strategy, tactics and lines that he used on me and the series of other women after; and the near irreparable destruction of my previous relationship, were some of the most instructive life lessons I have ever had. Did I mention that it took me over two years to accept my culpability in the entire episode? It was so easy to hate Tony for being a player, for not loving me, for me breaking up with Adam to be with him (though he never explicitly asked me to do that). The final exam in that life lesson came when I accepted that it was half my own damn fault: for not seeing what was in front of me; for accepting lies; for compromising my own happiness and blaming someone else; for hating someone for not loving me the way Adam did. Madness I know, but madness is more prevalent than we like to admit.

The next time I fell in lust, I also fell in love, and I fell in love first, with Yohan. What a beautiful and dangerous combination.

Why dangerous?

I believed in "destiny" and "true love" up to that point, and I thought I'd learned it all. So this combination of loving a person for who they are and them loving me for my brain and personality, along with the palpable sexual chemistry between us had to be IT! Believe me, I loved him and I believe in his own way he loved me, but we were not "meant" to be together.

The work that a relationship takes is shared equally by the partners and he was not ready at that time in his life - very early twenties - to do that work. I was only eighteen months older than he was, but the level of difference in our relationship maturity sometimes felt like a decade. Ironically, one of Yohan's most attractive features was his maturity. Along with it he had grace, pockets of wisdom and a genuine love and respect of women.

He wasn't perfect. He had a small problem with keeping his penis out of other women when I left the country; once I was in the country he was as loyal as they get. And here is where the irony continues; the sexual relationship we had was incomparable, on both sides. So along with the mental relationship, Yohan and I had a one-of-a-kind sexual relationship that could not, and maybe still cannot be replicated with anyone else. It was headboard banging, neighbours knocking, chair breaking, bed frame cracking, carpet burn inducing, sheet soaking, shower curtain ripping, tongues speaking, three times a night, all day on weekends and holidays, star-spangled sex. Yet Yohan, knowing that sexual infidelity was and is my deal breaker, gave it away when I was away.

We broke up; I was heartbroken and possibly a little mentally unstable for at least a year afterwards. I was still in love; but I had grown up enough to realise that being in love along with being in very compatible lust didn't make the relationship right. That long painful post-relationship period, inclusive of the "for old times' sake" sex and the eventual God-sent repatriation on my part was my research thesis in the lesson of self-love, romantic love and relationships that I had to learn.

I can clearly look at that relationship now and acknowledge that Yohan wasn't ready for the commitment I needed, that this didn't make him a bad person, and that it didn't make me unworthy of being loved. That didn't mean that I should sit around and wait for him to get to the stage I was at (I recently saw Agony Aunt "Dear Christine" give someone that advice). He had his life to live and his lessons to learn and I was there to help teach them, but I wasn't his final lesson - there is none really.

We're both now married to other people and have acknowledged that we were essential to each other in our self-defining early adult years. When I chose to be in a committed relationship again with my husband, it was a conscious decision based on the knowledge of how to coexist within a relationship, not the belief that lust and love were the guiding principles that defined THE ONE.

Dessert After The Dessert
Sandra Sealy

"Wuh's all dis?" he declared, looking up at me quizzically from the table.

"Just because."

A ray of a smile spread across his face. Then his knife and fork scraped the plate as he grunted his approval. He shook his head in amazement at each course being cleared.

Finally, the last dish was placed before him.

"So wuh is dis fuh dessert, sweetheart?" He asked, head tilted and glancing down at the menu.

"Looks like something new - an apple brandy tartlet," I smiled.

"Tastes real good, yeah."

With the Christmas tree barely whisked away and New Year's Eve champagne still lingering on my palate, along comes the next holiday to spend money (of which I had NONE) - Valentine's Day. Yes, it has grown commercial but I still think a day to focus on love is great.

I know I'm blessed. My man was so supportive that I couldn't even wait for the day when Cupid reigned supreme to celebrate. But who would've thought foreplay would've started a whole month in advance? Or even, that the real celebration would happen two weeks before February 14th?

Passion built over the course of the next few weeks.

It started with a tiny purple bloom (he obviously picked off someone's bush) that was presented to me with a flourish one evening. Then there were my playful pinches on his tight butt in passing, while he swatted me away in mock protest. On another occasion, I couldn't help but crack up at his hilarious soca strip tease. Even my naughty calls and texts to him at work knowing full well he couldn't respond...until he got home.

I wanted to make something special for dinner that night. He was particularly patient with me that week and I wanted to show my appreciation.

I scrounged around the cupboard and fridge for whatever I might find: chicken, the last of some broccoli florets, a bit of flour, some long-grained rice, pumpkin, six apples and thankfully, an untouched Christmas gift of zinfandel.

First, I put that bottle of wine in the fridge to chill, lime and salted the chicken, and then figured out what I would do with these ingredients. Just to keep track, I scribbled a list of what I planned to make.

Why not make it really different and forget the usual buffet, family style thing? So, I ended up printing a personalized four course à la carte menu for his place setting:

<u>Starter</u>
Tossed Salad With Mixed Greens
<u>Main</u>
Garlic Ginger Chicken With Herbed Rice And A Medley of Garden Vegetables
<u>Dessert</u>
Spiced Remy Martin Apple Tartlet
<u>Wine</u>
Zinfandel

Now it was time to cook everything from scratch. After a couple hours of chopping, blending, seasoning, rolling, stirring and baking, it was time to set the table with stemware, water glasses and cutlery.

I added lighted scented candles, cloth napkins and white tablecloth, soft, romantic music CDs and a bottle of wine, and voilà - I had created an instant "restaurant" on the cheap.

I dashed into the shower and while getting dressed, spritzed my pulse points with perfume. He would soon arrive.

***

After dinner, Remy Martin Cognac and romantic salsa music flowed as we reposed to the patio to chat and chuckle about our day. We hummed and tapped to a favourite familiar tune. Then I stood up and took his hand, "Let's dance."

We moved aside the footrest in the living room to make room for some rhumba, salsa and sexy bachata. Neither of us spoke Spanish, but we knew it was hot. Then came Enrique's track:

"Over and over I look in your eyes
you are all I desire
you have captured me
I want to hold you
I want to be close to you
I never want to let you go
I wish that this night would never end
I need to know…"

That said it all.

It was finally bedtime.

The high queen-sized bed stood centre stage with the top sheet expectantly peeled back. He closed the bedroom door.

We crawled into bed and dozed with the duvet-thick night surrounding us. The alcohol with the Latin music chaser from earlier that evening had set in and made us drowsy.

But I went to sleep with sweetness on my mind. My eyes fluttered open in the dark around 2:00 am. The sound of the wind was high through the slightly opened window.

The feel of a strong arm gently encircled me, like the diamond wedding band glittering on my left finger in the gloom.

Shifting slightly on my side, a smile swept across my face, at the familiar firm sign of welcome against my ass - even when he's fast asleep. The soldier in his pyjamas was always on duty. Stretching, my hips undulated slowly which seemed to wake him up.

As always, his fingers darted across the Braille of my steadily rising nipples. We both knew what was next in our timeless lateral duet. But somehow tonight was different.

Everyone likes vanilla ice cream. Though, as delightful as it is, vanilla ice cream everyday is what you'd expect: sweet, satisfying and you know exactly how it'll taste. So would it be possible to take it to another level?

Though we both wanted to satisfy our appetites, I playfully pushed him away. He sighed and lay on his back. I turned over and placed my ear on his chest to hear deep and even breathing in tune to the cadence of his heartbeat.

We chatted some more, and he complimented me again on the dinner. Somehow the talk turned to intimacy and the challenges of keeping a relationship fresh.

Lifting my head, I murmured, "You know when you have the roadmap to someone's body, sometimes it's good to try a new trail."

The time for talk was over.

Fingers gliding from his throat to his nipples below the forest of his hairy chest, made him shiver involuntarily. Then I stopped.

I need to put my money where my mouth is.

I sat up and threw the sheet off.

"Where you going?"

"Coming back now."

I padded into the kitchen and surveyed the bottom cupboard and grinned. Returning to the bedroom, I turned on a low light on the nightstand. I wanted him to see what I was doing.

Slowly, I shed my nightgown, maintaining eye contact.

"Wuh is dah?"

"Shhh...chocolate sauce. Just lay back and enjoy it.

With that, a thick, slow stream came spurting out of the bottle, which I drizzled from clavicle, along the middle of his chest and into his belly button. Anywhere that rivulet of chocolate went, lips and teeth and tongue followed.

Finally, I got all the way downtown, long minutes after involuntary trembling and begging.

Arms, torso and legs shuddered like Mount Vesuvius about to erupt. His loud, almost strangled moans, filled the shadowed room as I painstakingly devoured *my* dessert...after the apple tart.

"Oh my God!" he panted in the aftermath. Then he lovingly tortured *me* by returning the favour.

No doubt, after more than ten years of marriage - especially during middle age - embracing the exploration of sensuality, is a sweet gift.

Kissing Frogs
Aubrey Edwards

Early on Valentine's Day, I already felt like I was walking on air. My boyfriend Logan's greeting card had arrived in the mail that morning and he had expressed in great detail what he loved about me and our relationship.

When I went to work, I noticed all eyes were on me as I entered the building. *That's strange*, I thought to myself. My co-worker Michelle, who shares an office with me, pointed her smartphone in my direction. It took me a few seconds to notice the bouquet of flowers sitting on my desk.

I giggled like an excited schoolgirl and I could feel my face flush. More co-workers rushed into my office to catch a glimpse of my reaction. As it turned out, Logan had orchestrated the surprise with Michelle as his accomplice. She was recording my initial shock since he couldn't be there to enjoy it.

"Thank you, baby! I love you," I said into the camera after shooing away my overly curious co-workers. This was our first Valentine's Day and we weren't even in the same country.

We are both devoted to our long distance relationship because Logan and I are a good match for each other. Along with the obvious chemistry, shared interests and values, and similar sense of humour, Logan and I just work. When we first started hanging out, we felt so natural that we both knew pretty quickly that we were going to be together. He's the first man who made me comfortable enough to be completely myself. His maturity and level-headedness balance out my anxiety and scatterbrained tendencies when I'm under a lot of stress.

Logan also happens to be a white American man (well, he identifies as half-white but more on that later). Not the first white guy I've dated but the first man of any colour I've been serious about.

I had to kiss a whole lot of frogs before I met Logan. Unfortunately, most of them were black; black Bajans to be specific. These men were an interesting mix of personalities with varying levels of attractiveness and sex appeal. And most of them treated me like crap.

Before I get hate mail for being a "Bajan basher", let me explain. Like many girls growing up in Barbados, I didn't have the healthiest relationship with my father, who actually lived in another country. When Bajan pundits complain about fatherless children, they tend to focus exclusively on the lack of male role models for young boys and completely ignore how equally damaging it is for their sisters not to have a fully engaged father. You don't need a Psychology degree to know that girls often end up dating men who are just like their fathers, whether they like it or not.

So, from my teenage years to my early 20s, I was always drawn to emotionally unavailable men who only showed mild romantic interest in me. Even though in Bajan society there is a pervasive acceptance of philandering and lack of respect for women, I don't completely blame the frogs for my shitty romantic history. The sexist Bajan culture, my insecurities and my glaring daddy issues just happen to make the perfect recipe for a disastrous pattern of relationships. One paramour dumped me because he was "too busy for a relationship" but he was engaged to another girl less than a year later. (Was he seeing us at the same time?)

An ex-boyfriend was bitter that I made him take me out for dinner on Valentine's Day because he'd rather go to a beer lime at UWI with his buddies. Bear in mind, that I agreed to TGI Friday's, not the most romantic setting. He spent the whole evening bitching about his overpriced burger.

Another ex spread rumours about me on campus, saying that I was an idiot who wouldn't leave him alone. Meanwhile, to my face he told me I was a great girlfriend and he was in love with me. I don't advocate domestic violence but when I cuffed that guy after dumping him, he muttered he deserved it.

When I moved to Philadelphia during my mid-20s for graduate school, I saw this as an opportunity for a fresh start. It was a foreign city where no one knew me and I could leave my baggage behind in Barbados. The thing about personal baggage is that it tends to follow you wherever you go unless you figure out how to manage it. You may never be issue-free but at least you can lessen the load.

Nevertheless, I think the change of scenery and distance from my toxic memory-filled stomping grounds allowed me to open up my baggage and slowly discard the mental garbage that was plaguing me. Low self-worth - torn to shreds. Burden of a dysfunctional relationship history - tossed aside. Daddy issues - well, I still carry them around but they've gotten a lot lighter.

This unloading of luggage, of course, did not happen overnight, more like three years or so. And along the way, I still encountered dirt bags in Philly but each one was less awful than the previous. And I learned to approach each romantic failure as a lesson and not as an ugly blemish on my self-image.

Now, I'm not going to be completely dishonest and pretend I wasn't drawn to the allure of dating guys of other ethnicities when moving to Philadelphia. There were some positive stereotypes that I wanted to explore for myself. More than one cousin told me to snag a white guy because "they treat their women good". A few friends swore by the passion of the latino lover. Another friend insisted "Indian men don't cheat". Meanwhile, my mother quietly hoped I'd "just meet someone". When I first arrived, I decided to have an open mind.

One of my first suitors in Philadelphia was an African American named Duane and I was done with him within a week. When I first met him in a hair salon, I was attracted to his dark, smooth complexion, buffed physique as well as his swagger. Unfortunately, he fit every stereotype in the book! He had a child out of wedlock with a "spiteful" girlfriend he dumped while she was pregnant. Baby mama drama! He couldn't understand why I would want to move back to little old, backwards Barbados. His idea of a first date was to ditch the barbecue we were supposed to attend together and invite me to his sister's ghetto street party. He had very narrow ideas about what black people should and should not enjoy. (Black kids skateboarding? The horror!) And when he learned a white man was also interested in me, his logical response was to declare he had a bigger dick that could do the job, sending me photographic evidence along with his testimony.

I blacklisted African American men for two years because of him! I knew it wasn't fair to appoint Duane as the ambassador of all African Americans but since he was my first one and was worse than any Bajan guy I'd been with, I was determined to taste other delicacies.

There's some truth to the passionate latino cliché but proponents of this usually forget to mention that many of these Spanish lovers are bigger womanisers than Bajan men! I met my Venezuelan boyfriend through a mutual friend. He was cute, short and chubby, and his Hispanic accent accentuated his charm. We had intense chemistry and I got caught up in a whirlwind affair. It abruptly ended when he confessed that he cheated on me with his ex...right after I treated him to a birthday dinner.

The big shocker for my friends and my mother was my summer fling with a white Republican named Dave. Many people would label me as a liberal so that, along with the not-so-subtle racism associated with this political group, made this pairing surprising for most. It didn't help that he was divorced, older and balding, not my usual type. Nonetheless, I was drawn to his easy-going nature and he convinced me that politics wasn't enough of a reason not to give him a chance. I had fun but everything fell apart when it became apparent that Dave wasn't comfortable with an opinionated liberal woman. This romance was short-lived but Dave treated me with respect and dating him felt like a step forward in the right direction. I believed I was on my way to a healthier relationship now that I held higher standards for myself.

After living in Philadelphia for a couple years, I decided to give another black American a chance. I won't lie. Part of the reason I dated Bob was because his parents were Haitian. This is significant if you're aware of black American culture. There's a rift between Caribbean Americans and African Americans, mostly because of a difference in culture and values. African Americans had to deal with a much longer history of intense oppression and segregation. So African Americans tend to come off as if they're trying to create an identity for themselves as minorities whereas Caribbean Americans have a stronger sense of culture that's not tied to being "different" to white people.

Getting back to my first black American friend Duane...this was what helped me quickly realize it couldn't work. Duane felt special because he was going to college whereas in Barbados that's very common. He thought rock music was only for whites, except for Linkin Park because they incorporate rap into their style. I enjoy rock music and I have many black friends who do too. He was horrified that black kids were starting to wear Converse and I'm sure many Bajans didn't even consider that a "white thing". I just couldn't relate to restricting my interests and tastes to fit into the "black club".

Unfortunately, Haitian American Bob wasn't as Caribbean as I hoped. He was open-minded about certain things but he grew up in the infamous West Philadelphia neighbourhood and bought into some aspects of ghetto culture. He was a gentleman at first, but I ended it when he started to treat me like a hood rat.

At that point I had given up hope of meeting someone worthwhile in Philadelphia. Although I had made some wonderful friends, I was homesick and fed up with the crummy weather. I finished school; I quit my job and made plans to move back to Barbados. Six weeks before my flight home, mutual friends set me up with Logan. We connected right away but I kept pushing him away. I didn't see the point in getting attached when I was leaving so soon.

Thankfully, Logan didn't give up on me and he prevailed. We liked each other so much that it soon became apparent to both of us a long distance relationship was inevitable. Things are going really well despite the thousands of miles between us. He respects my opinions, feelings, and values as well as my culture; I think this multicultural acceptance stems from his background – German/Puerto Rican American.

Logan's the most romantic guy I've ever dated. He always makes me feel special and appreciated, whether it's the traditional route of sending flowers on Valentine's Day or a more creative gesture, such as a love note in the form of a puzzle I have to piece together.

I don't want my story to be an argument for why black Bajan women should date white men. I just think my path is an example of why we should have an open mind to interracial dating. I know it's a cliché to say you have to kiss a lot of frogs to get to the prince but there's truth to that. However, I would alter that adage to say kissing all those frogs (of many colours) helps you to appreciate the prince when you meet him.

OVERCOMING ABUSE

Diary of a Punching Bag
Jackie Jones

<u>Early 2004</u>

"Look at me," he said grasping my shoulders, "Don't ever let me hear you say you're worthless again." I remember that day and those words clearly. We were sitting in his car, which he had stopped abruptly as he tried to make me see how important I was. As he tried to make me believe I was special.

We were just friends then, interested in each other for no other reason than the music we made together and the jokes and stories shared. At least, that's what I thought. I had no idea that this man, ten years my senior, had other plans altogether. He'd seen the insecurities that I kept hidden from others and was already plotting the ways he would exploit each and every one to his advantage.

At first it was the little things, like making me think that my boyfriend at the time wasn't really into me. He'd feed me all kinds of tales that I believed because I thought he was just being a good friend. And, though that relationship would probably have been short-lived either way, he definitely helped to hurry the process along. Next he attacked my family, whispering deep into my ear about their lack of support as it related to my music. As for my friends, well, that came later, but let's just say that according to him, every guy friend wanted to screw me and every girlfriend secretly hated me.

When we got together some months later, I thought I was doing the right thing. Even though he wasn't physically my type, he'd always been good to me and encouraged me when I thought no one else cared. He was my knight in shining armour and I didn't see the dents until it was way too late.

<u>Late 2004</u>

It started with a bite. I'd gotten very angry at him one night and for the first time he retaliated. Usually he didn't, which served to make me angrier and I sometimes lashed out, fists acting maliciously against wide biceps before I could stop myself. I screamed, I shouted, I did all kinds of things in those early months, until I realised that I couldn't be that person. So I started trying to curb my quick temper.

However, that night something silly had happened. I don't even remember what it was. It's funny how I seldom remember what fuelled his violent reactions, just the actions themselves; this time it was a bite. He grabbed my arm as I screamed at him and clamped viciously down with his mouth, tearing flesh with his uneven teeth. I was shocked and moments later ran to the telephone to call my mother, to tell her what he had done. As I explained to her, in a calmer voice than one would imagine, my story turned into a lie, as I assured her - panic lacing her tone - that I'd just been kidding around. This decision was one of the earlier mistakes.

Realising that I wasn't going to out him for his animal-like behaviour, he started getting bolder. He pushed me against walls and doors, cornered me so I couldn't get away and held my arms tightly in his own so I couldn't move. This was his training ground and he was just getting started. He'd tasted my blood and now whenever he was angry, was delirious for it. He loved the scent of my fear and preyed upon it. He wanted more and he was going to take it in any way he could.

2005

Slowly I became lost in this new culture that was my life. If I gave into my anger, I was met with a kind of violence that I'd wish on no one. He never broke bones or left visible marks in obvious places, no, he was much smarter than that, but he hurt me in ways that I didn't think were possible. Not for *me*, not Jackie who had once stood up to a guy angrily wielding a large stone. Not *Jackie*, who not once, but *twice* had tried her best to help other girls in abusive relationships. But, it *was* me.

I looked into the mirror daily, starting to see the shell of my past self, the real me, left behind in favour of its submissive counterpart, terrified whenever his anger entered the room. Especially because it came along with a host of inanimate objects that played the game just as well as he did.

Who would have thought that a frying pan could hold such power, or even a broomstick? Both, by the way, have already been broken on my body. I'd often fall to the floor when he went into his rages, my instincts urging me to live another day. I was a tortured ball of flesh and bone on the floor of his apartment, hating him, but knowing what had to be done for it to stop…

"I love you, I'm sorry," I'd say over and over, my voice sometimes no more than a frightened whimper over the shouting and spit that rained down with the blows. He didn't stop otherwise; why would he? I was his punching bag and he wasn't nearly done.

Late 2006

After each "kickboxing" session, I'd feel myself go just a little more numb inside. I'd feel hurt and pain that would own me from my head to feet and yet, I would pull myself together to comfort him. He'd be sitting quietly, saying nothing, the pain of what he'd done too much for him to bear. In the beginning I thought that was it, I even scoured all kinds of educational resources, believing that he fell into blind rages. Now, I know way better.

He manipulated me without so much as a nudge from Harry's wand. He knew what he was doing, every step he took, every word he said, every blow he administered. He wasn't a sad man disgusted with himself for his behaviour, oh no, he was a man who knew the woman he was with. He knew I'd comfort him and saw it as the easiest way to win my favour again. And so I'd worm my way into his arms, ignoring his struggle to keep me out and sit on his lap, hugging him, kissing, cooing softly that it was okay. After all, I wasn't dead was I?

When enough time had passed, he'd open back up, tears, if you can believe it, lodged in his eyes. He'd hug me tight, "sorry" the buzzword and later, if I was *really* good, I might even get a gift as another way to make it up to me. Yes, he covered every one of his bases. He left no stone unturned and with every fresh beating, which could either come every other day or maybe every couple weeks, he'd find new ways to harm me and just as easily, new ways to win back my affection.

Early 2007

By year three, I'd had more than enough. My transition into numb-mode was nearly complete and even the violence became something like the norm for me.

When it happened, it simply did. The few people that knew about it, acted as though they were horrified whenever I'd tell them but for me, it was no big deal. This was just how the other half lived, no biggie.

Maybe if it was just the physical things, I would have left sooner, who knows, but this man attacked every part of my psyche. When I looked really great, to him I looked like a whore, when I did very well onstage, he would compliment me sure, but would always make sure he told me about *someone* who thought I was absolutely awful. He didn't like the idea of anyone getting too close to me either and continued to play on my quest to be a good girlfriend, in order to secure his claim.

He was relentless in his task. He wanted to crush me and so he tried and succeeded for a time. The thoughts in my head became so dark, that though I'd take it all with little reprisal, sometimes I'd look at him and imagine sliding a knife across his neck, watching him bleed from ear to ear. It made me smile to think these things and when I caught myself, when I realised that I was allowing another human being to bring me to the brink of madness, I knew that something had to be done.

Mid-2007

Instead of murder, I started plotting my escape. No, I didn't live with him and could leave when I wanted - unless he didn't want me to of course, but leaving a relationship like that *does* require some thought and cunning. I was prisoner to his whims and fancies. Attacked on one occasion in such a terrifying way, that I thought I would lose my life, all for one reason - I wouldn't have sex with him. So yes, I had to *plot* my escape.

He held the band we were in together hostage, telling me that he would not be a part of it should I leave him. Another manipulation I know now, but then it was easy to fall into these traps. I tried other ways, threatening involving the police, to which he once replied, "Whenever I get out of jail, I'll come and kill your whole family."

Sounds like something from the movie *Taken*, but this was no cinematic experience; this was my life and I was completely scared. He terrorized, coerced, manipulated and attacked, whatever worked and I knew that if I were to break those bonds that held me, I'd need more than words.

An opportunity presented itself just after the summer of the fourth year of our sham of a relationship. A longtime friend, who he'd never liked, asked me to meet him. My friend was feeling low after breaking up with his girlfriend and wanted a familiar ear to share his drama with. I informed my "master" of this new development and he became very upset, so as was customary, I decided fine, I wouldn't go. Only, I did.

<u>Late 2008</u>

It wasn't really a lie at the time. I had really chosen not to go, but after thinking about it for a while longer decided screw it, I was going to help my friend, whether he liked it or not. You must understand that by this time, I was starting to recapture a shadow of my defiant spirit and though my stomach churned as I thought of his reaction on the bus ride there, I did not turn back.

After a few hours of spending time with my friend, the boyfriend called. He was livid when he found out where I was, called me all manner of vile names as he was prone to do and then, broke up with me for the hundredth time. Now, he was always breaking up with me for a few hours then coming back after I'd begged him to. Another manipulation, yes, I see it now. It had become an annoyance to me as well and I'd often said to him that one day, the yo-yo wouldn't bounce back.

On that night, as I sat listening to him rant, I made my decision and when he called me later on, telling me he was sorry and we could get back together I said,

"No."

This of course threw him off-track and he had no idea what to do. He tried all the usual tricks, but I refused to budge, "numbing down" - as I like to call it - as much as was necessary so I wouldn't retract my decision. He hated it and I loved this new power I was feeling as I took a real stand for the first time in years. But, it wasn't over quite yet.

<u>December 2008 (Evening)</u>

Despite the breakup, our band's activities continued for a little while, but he could not stand that I wouldn't get back together with him. He was still verbally abusive, sometimes calling me more awful names in a minute than most have probably been called in a lifetime. He would repeatedly curse me, dare me to talk back to him and be overall a horrible person towards me whenever he had the chance.

It all came to a head one evening just before rehearsal. I'd been particularly annoyed at something and had been dropping little passive aggressive comments at every turn. Eventually, he got so angry that he struck back.

First, he jumped on the bed where I was sitting and

started to punch me repeatedly in my head. When the bassist of the band pulled him off me, trying to get him to cool off and holding onto him so he couldn't come after me again, everything seemed as if it would be okay, but he wasn't finished. The moment he was released, nodding when asked if he was okay, he sprang at me again, this time biting at my face, while hitting me wherever he could, over and over.

I felt my body go limp, lying there in a kind of foetal position and it was as if I stopped breathing. It was so strange and something I'd never want to experience again. It was as if my body was saving me from itself, keeping me safe until it was all over.

<u>December 2008 (Evening Continued)</u>

When I wouldn't move, it seemed that he became afraid and raised himself up a bit, calling my name repeatedly, but I wouldn't answer. He told everyone to get out of the room or he'd hurt me more and, fearing for my safety, they agreed. He continued to call out my name and, as if I'd lost my voice, I still didn't respond. Finally, probably fearing that he'd gone too far and killed me, he said,

"Answer me or I'll hit you again." Yes, this was my life.

When he'd said that a few more times and I could feel him gearing up to do just that, I stirred, not sure that my bruised body could take much more. I got up and tried to move away from him and he, realising that I would be okay, got up too, moving away to get his "instruments". You see, he was a cutter too - only it was superficial. He did it as a way to manipulate me into feeling bad for him when he was the one doing wrong.

Don't believe me? Think I'm insensitive? Well, usually when you're a cutter, I assume you wouldn't use dull blades as he did.

This man controlled my life and actions for all this time and here it was that even in a situation where he'd obviously gone far overboard with me, he still could not help taking all the attention for himself. And me, still wanting the best, tried to make him stop "cutting" with the dull, ridiculous, blade.

2014

I'm still not over every element of that time and getting past those things that I am, was hard. It was a process made more difficult as he spread awful rumours about me and even shared personal things about my life with people I didn't even know.

However, I have grown and learnt from the experience. What makes me happiest is that even though our relationship was so plagued with horrid moments, I haven't lumped all men into this category. I know there are good ones out there and have met a couple in the last years whom I have loved deeply.

Single now, I know that someday when the time proves right, I'll find another who is worthy of the love and affection I'm willing to give. For now though, words are my passion, family and friends my heart, - and punching bags? Well, if they are not in a gym or maybe a backyard for personal use, if they're not filled with sand, if they're you - know that despite how things may seem, despite what anyone says, you are strong enough to overcome. I was strong enough. I survived and I still have room for love and someone new in my life.

Humans are resilient beings and women, most of all.

Going Home
Katherine Felix

Even in the dark, I know I am home from the weight of the mountains which surround me as I step off the plane. The moist lushness of the rainforests nearby seems to have substance, and like a child wrapped in warm blankets, I feel the mountains enfold me as the lilt of creole accents combine with the song of the frogs and a peace settles down in me.

Home.

I had been too tight on funds to make a trip home in over six months. I hadn't realized how much I needed the little recharge until now. As much as I love Barbados, there is something about St Lucia that replenishes my soul, and I was overdue for a top-up.

I take a deep breath of the sea-soaked atmosphere on Vigie beach before getting into the rental car, which is inundated with the moist, humid scent of volcanoes and Caribs; both long dormant here but still alive in my imaginings.

I have no set agenda for this trip, and since it's close to the airport, on a whim I turn onto Sans Soucci, headed towards the best hugger and my spiritual sparring partner, Ski. For conversation, creative blessings, and the best massage in the universe, Ski has always been the one I could turn to. He saw me through the death of my son and John's addiction. We both went through the collapse of our marriages at the same time.

Pulling up in front of the house, local music blaring

away on the radio of my rental car, Ski will definitely know someone is there. As usual, there is a gathering on the front balcony of the house. There must have been at least five guys probably passing a joint from one to the next on a long wooden bench. All eyes are on me as I get out of the car, a white chick in a rental car; headed straight for Ski and my hug. A wave of amusement passes through me as I imagine the high musings as each of the fellows comes up with their own interpretation of who I am and what I am doing here. In the dark, I can't make out the individuals but I feel the eyes on me. I put them out of my mind as Ski came out to greet me, his smile warming my spirit. A mirrored smile was etched on my own face, stretching every muscle in my cheeks, and it's obvious from the stretch in some of the seldom used facial muscles, that I don't smile like this very often.

"Gal, I didn't expect to see you round here any time soon. How are you? How is Barbados treating you?" he asks in his reggae voice, as his strong brown arms reach to enfold me in a deep, warm, long hug. A hug that removes all the work stress, travelling on LIAT stress… and just like that, I feel like a skin has been shed and I am myself again.

I take a step back, still holding on, arm to arm; "Just stopped by on a whim Ski, following my heart where it leads me as always. And it led to your door straight from the airport."

I become conscious of someone to the right of me, on the porch, watching me so intently that I can feel the stare, so I turn to look and see who it is.

"Jah". The word is out of my mouth before I realize it. "Jaws, that's you?"

My ex-husband is right there, sitting on Ski's porch,

fidgeting like he wants to leave but unable to do so without getting closer to me than he already is. Disconcerted, I never let go of my grip on Ski. I had not seen John in over eight years.

Damned if he didn't look good.

It was as if the man I fell in love with all those years ago had risen from the dead. The last time I saw him that would have been a fairly good description: one of the walking dead; a jumbie.

The last five years that I was living in St. Lucia, John had been in prison. I had divorced him legally, about two and a half years before. But that was strictly because of financial constraints. The marriage had been over since shortly after our son died during delivery and John's addiction killed off what little was left afterwards. The year he went to jail he had lost his mother, and whatever self-control he had managed to muster to be functional died with her.

"Yea it's me."

The baritone sound of his voice took me back to a million memories all at once. Some good, some bad, many just sad.

Although my composure was shaken, I still couldn't help but smile.

"You look good John. I just came over from Barbados and thought I would stop and say hello to Ski, so let me do that and I'll talk to you in a few."

I kicked my shoes off while moving Ski backwards into his living room. We had never broken contact from the hug; he had been my equilibrium throughout the brief exchange in the doorway. From the corner of my eye I had registered all the expressions passing over his face from amusement to concern to care and understanding.

He ushered me around to the couch. The room has not changed since my last visit months ago: the same crushed velvet red and orange cushions, knickknacks and books from years ago fill the bookshelf/room divider, the television front and centre, playing nothing to attract my focus.

As we sat, John stuck his head around the edge of the front door. I was surprised that I could still read hurt and anger in his eyes so easily. "Katherine, I have some papers by Daddy that belong to you. Check me before you leave so I can give them to you."

Abruptly, with back rigid, shoulders slumped, he turned and left while I am still saying, "Okay, sure John, no problem."

When he leaves, the tension goes with him and I exhale a breath I didn't realize I was holding, turning to look at Ski.

"Garcion, you could not tell me the man was out of jail? Jah knows I didn't need to find out so."

"Girl I meant to tell you, I just didn't think that I would be seeing you tonight. That was something else though," he says, smiling a knowing, sarcastic smile. I reach out and hit him lightly on the shoulder, frowning, but followed by my own smile.

"He looks, I don't know, clean. He has on jewelry. Is he…is he using?"

"I think he is good, but then only he and Jah know that for sure. He has been home about six weeks Kat. He says he struggles still, every day; but he seems to have gotten some help at Bordelais, and he is definitely trying. Keynon fixed him up a little apartment at the back of the garage; he does odd jobs in the neighbourhood and seems to be staying away from temptation. He is here most days, and we vibe. I reason with him. His head is still messed up with prison life, but he's coming along, for now."

I try to get my bearings and settle into a normal flow of conversation with Ski, but my mind keeps seeing the emotions in John's face as he left for his father's and eventually both Ski and I admit what we both know; that I am not fully able to concentrate on catching up and sharing life stories. I promise to get back to see him the following day, and head down the block to my father-in-law's house to find John. I imagine the houses in the neighbourhood all having eyes peeping from behind each window as I walk past them. St Lucia is small and news travels fast. The gossip mill in Sans Soucci will have enough fodder to run all weekend.

I make an impromptu decision to carry him out to dinner, catch up with him and see for myself who he is, and how he is first hand. There has always been a part of me praying for him to find the strength to rise above that damn addiction, hoping he would find his way back to himself. A part of me never believed in that miracle, but I guess my heart is forever optimistic.

I offered and he accepted.

During the drive up north, he complained: "you didn't even look at me when you came up the stairs to Ski's."

That explained why he had been upset. "You pulled up to the house and never even noticed me. My wife who he hasn't seen me in years, pulls up to my friends' house. I was sitting there watching you, recognizing you before you were out of the car, but you never even acknowledged my presence until after hugging another man. Never mind it was Ski."

I wanted to laugh, it was such an irrational complaint, but he was being honest and admitting what he felt without malice or subterfuge, and I didn't want to dishonour that.

I just explained that I hadn't seen him, which was useless of course because as far as he was concerned that was the issue - I should have "felt" his presence and known it was him, just as he had known it was me.

The papers from his father's house turned out to be the divorce papers I served him while he was in prison. He had refused to sign them, but said if I still wanted the divorce he understood and would sign the papers for me now. I got a sinking feeling on hearing that since we already were divorced and he was obviously never informed by the court. Now I got to tell him. Oh *Joy*.

"John, there was a hearing. You were supposed to have been given legal counsel and transport to Castries from the prison to attend the court session. It was horrible, waiting for you to show up. I sat there in the courtroom, sweating and nervous, expecting you to come in and fight the divorce but since you never turned up, the divorce was granted."

The reality is that we had not been man and wife in more than ten years in my heart or any meaningful or physical manner. We had been legally divorced for almost three years and he did not even know it until this night. What a crappy way to start the conversation. I felt on the defence and guilty, even though I had nothing to feel guilty about.

I fully expected that we would soon be arguing and the dinner would be a very short one, but I was wrong. There was a part of us both that needed to say everything that had not been said, to hear each other, and somehow it worked.

We talked about everything: the addiction, financial hardships, and loss of material possessions, starting over, friends and the broken relationships between him and the kids. We skirted the subject for a while, and both ended up in tears when we finally could go around it no longer and the ghost of our son came to rest between us. And we both blamed ourselves and each other. Somehow, that made it a little less horrible.

"It was your fault, damn it."

Those words that were never spoken at the time, the ones we ate and choked on, while trying to salvage a marriage we both believed in when we said "I do".

Perhaps it was that we had nothing left to lose and there was a bond between us spanning twenty-five years, originally grounded in love and mutual respect.

We had this night, this unexpected moment, and while dinner came and went, dessert, then coffee. Other diners left one by one. We healed.

John cost me everything I worked for, everything we both worked for, in the first thirty-two years of our lives. His addiction wiped out everything and I was left in a country that didn't like foreigners and two children to raise on my own. I started over there twice - first with him, then afterwards on my own with the kids.

He manipulated my emotions when we were together, and made me feel as though his habit was caused by my inadequacies and mistakes. Not that I was perfect or I didn't make mistakes, but I was blamed for his actions and wanted to hate him, but was never able to. All these years had passed with these things buried in me.

On this rare night, a moment was gifted to us both.

In this very special, unexpected evening, John looked at me and apologized.

He looked in my eyes, his own filled with tears, and took the responsibility that he had laid at my feet over and over during our marriage. He lightened my heart, one word at a time and his own heart lightened along with mine. If anyone tells you there is no magic in the world, tell them I say they lie.

All the grief, resentment and pain I bore for so long; things I thought I had gotten over years before; fell from me, and as I let the tears roll down my cheeks, I remembered, not the jumbie, not the man lost under an addiction, but I could see the glimmer of the man I fell in love with before he fell in love with drugs. I am not sure who benefited more from the evening, but I know that when I eventually dropped him back home and hugged him good night, I was not the same person who stepped off that plane a few short hours before and he was not the same man who was jealous of one of his best friends hugging his "wife".

Miracles do happen. Addicts can recover and love. Love can do amazing things, even when it cannot be resurrected.

You can go home again.

Crowded
Vanessa Carrington

I've always heard little pockets of complaints about having to deal with the shenanigans of a "child mother", but nothing could prepare me for what I experienced.

My best friend Tamara and I were stuck inside the library for hours, struggling to finish an assignment due the next day. She pointed at a guy sitting in the corner. "He can help," she insisted, "they've all been getting help from him." Being desperate, I walked over and awkwardly explained that I was in one of his classes.

His eyebrows softened and his lips curled into a smile. It was nice. He had light brown skin, with black, curly hair and perfectly straight, white teeth. "I know who you are," he said. "Your name is Vanessa and I'm Nathan, and yes I can help."

It is so funny how you could sit in the same classroom as someone for several weeks and never notice them, but once you have been introduced, they become the first thing you see when you enter that same room.

We became friends.

With each conversation I learned something more about him. He was single and had a six-month old baby boy. He was a proud Dad, showing me dozens of baby pictures saved in his phone.

The day I finally met the baby's mother soon came screeching around the corner. Until then, I hadn't thought much of her. I knew they were together from high school, she was his first and that they had broken up before she found out she was pregnant. He told me they were only communicating for the sake of the baby, and so I didn't feel like I needed to know much more than that. At that time, I still thought of him as just a friend from school.

That afternoon, Nathan, Tamara and I were studying for exams at his house. The sharp steady buzz of the doorbell broke our concentration, and he left us to answer the door. Tamara and I continued our chatter, unaware of what was happening in another room.

"Shhh, be quiet, you hearing that?" asked Tamara. I stopped immediately and tried to listen. Both of us were silent, with wrinkled foreheads, tuning our ears to pick up the now slightly elevated discussion inside the living room. Then without warning, heavy footsteps started towards us, and as they grew louder and closer, the more nervous I became.

Then there she was, standing by the doorway, blocking any chance of escape.

My fear may have made her bigger than she actually was. She glared at us through cold, angry eyes. Beads of sweat trickled down her flustered face, and pooled around her neck. Strands of her straightened hair had eased its way out of the ruffle that was holding it in a loose ponytail. Her eyes went back and forth, from one of us to the next, down towards the books and papers scattered all over the floor, and finally back up to us. Her chunky arms moved from its previous position in her chubby waistline and now were straight at her sides. She balled her hands into a tight fist.

In all that time neither of us moved.

Finally, after what seemed like an eternity, we heard Nathan's voice from behind her outside the door. "Shanice, what is your problem?"

She turned without even taking a second glance and walked away. Moments later, we heard the door to the house slam shut.

Very little was said about that exchange as we all tried to go back to studying. Three hours later, when we were taking a break from the books and just wasting time with idle chatter, Nathan's phone rang. He looked, frowning, at the caller ID and answered the phone.

"Yeah." There was a long pause and he looked at us. He sighed and then responded with another yes. Suddenly Nathan moved the phone quickly away from his ear, his face winced at the loud blast coming from his phone. Now we all could hear the screaming female voice on the other end, wanting to know why those bitches were still there and why he hadn't thrown them out yet. Tamara obviously found this quite amusing because she burst out laughing.

This only served to get Shanice even angrier than she already was. She yelled that Tamara and I were skanks and that she should come back down there and beat us. "Come back down here to beat us then, see if I don't tie those two big bubbies in a bow for you," Tamara replied.

Shanice had no clue which one of us had said that, so automatically she chose one.

I was the lucky winner.

After that encounter, I should have run as far away as I could in the other direction, but I didn't.

Nathan and I were really getting close. I felt once I said or did nothing to poke the beast then nothing bad should happen. So, I avoided going to his house when there was a chance she could show up and we mostly saw each other at school. All was going to plan until he thought it would be a good idea to tell Shanice that he developed a serious interest in me, and was going to make me his girlfriend.

Bad idea!

She argued with him for over an hour, insisting that I was not right for him and I certainly was not right to be around her child. Because of her reaction, I decided it was best I left Nathan but he was not willing to let me go so easily. He convinced me that it could work and I wanted to believe him.

In the following days and weeks, I had to endure all kinds of rude remarks from her. She made it her life's mission to meddle in my business. She snooped around, found out who were my friends, and even my enemies! She dug around in my past and reported everything she found back to Nathan. I was privy to all my indiscretions as they were told to me one by one, from the lips of my new lover. She even added her own spice to my stories to make them sound so much more scandalous.

One evening, I came upon Shanice and the baby in town and she said she needed money to get home as she was broke. I immediately gave her bus fare to get home, even though she was being mean to me. I hoped that with my small kind gesture that she would see that I'm not trying to cause problems.

Unfortunately, later that night, she continued her rampage of complete desecration of my character.

Every new complaint I had to sit through made me boil little by little inside. For weeks I had to listen to people asking me who was this girl Shanice that kept questioning them about me and claiming that I was saying bad things about her to her son's father.

I was really getting sick of her snooping, judgment and lies, but still I held on, thinking that with time and some support from him, this could work. I believed that if she saw that I was not going to get in the way of him spending time with their son, that she would eventually stop making me a priority in her life.

This was not to be.

On one occasion that I will never forget, Nathan and I spent the day at the beach. We made other plans to go out later that same day, so it was easier for me to bathe and change at his house, and I accidentally left my brassiere in his bathroom. A couple days later, I had the displeasure of being sent a photo of Shanice wearing my brassiere, and posing with a smile. I was furious!

One day Nathan confessed to me that deep down inside, he did not think that the child belonged to him. He expressed how ashamed he felt for feeling this way, wanting to get a paternity test and he wouldn't blame me if I felt disgusted. I simply told him if finding out for sure will give him peace of mind then perhaps he should consider that avenue.

When he told Shanice he wanted a paternity test, she completely lost it. She told everyone that would listen, including his mother and aunts, that I placed doubts in his head about their child in an effort to yank him away from raising their son. From that moment onward, his family disliked me.

One Friday evening, I was at his house sitting and watching wrestling, when the doorbell rang.

It was Shanice.

She had come to drop off the baby because she wanted to go out partying that night, and he had agreed to babysit. However, when she saw me sitting there she was very unhappy.

She walked in, put down the baby and baby bag, mumbling her disapproval. All the while they were arguing I sat there, pretending not to notice someone else was even in the room. I figured she would just get bored and leave. Nathan, maybe looking for a quick way to end the dispute simply said, "I change my mind, I'm not keeping him anymore." As he started to gather up the baby and baby bag, she turned around and walked through the door, into the night. He followed her with their bundle of joy.

My curiosity soon got the better of me and I went outside to see what was happening. She realized he was on her trail and she sped up. Eventually he caught up to her and more arguing and gesturing occurred. They were now too far away for me to hear what they were saying but I could tell they weren't exchanging pleasantries.

He outstretched his hand to give her the bag and she allowed it to slide to the ground. He decided he would try this same thing with their baby expecting different results.

He was wrong.

The baby slid onto the road.

In complete disbelief, I walked back inside the house and sat down. Five minutes later, Nathan came back inside without the baby or the bag. Then there was a loud BUP.

Shanice had thrown a brick at the windshield of his car and ran down the road.

We discussed the madness for about forty-five minutes, only to be interrupted by police sirens and flashing lights. Shanice had called the police and made a complaint saying that Nathan dropped their child in the road. She was outside, screaming at the top of her lungs over and over, "HE GOT A WOMAN IN THERE, HE GOT A WOMAN IN THERE!"

The policemen soon caught on to the real issue and spoke to both of them calmly about being responsible parents, despite their separation and the fact that he had moved on. They left the premises, but their presence had already alerted the neighbours and Nathan's family.

There was only so much I could take. After two years, I finally packed up and left.

A year later, my cell phone rang. I recognized Nathan's number.

"Hello."

"The DNA test came back and he isn't mine!"

"What?!"

I was caught completely off guard. I was in shock.

He repeated the statement, and I could hear the pain and hurt in his voice. It is only after we hung up and I sat there thinking, and replaying everything in my mind, that I felt the anger.

It was as if I went through all of that drama for absolutely nothing.

Thanks to her, my back is a lot broader, and each moment taught me that I was a stronger person than I knew myself to be. Moving forward, and trusting someone again after that experience was hard, but I learnt that for a relationship to work, both parties need to be committed to each other, and ignore outside influences.

Three people cannot be in a relationship together.

My Guardian Angel
Tricia B.

It started with a simple Facebook message: "Hi, my name is Daphne, and I'm a Barbadian aspiring writer based in London. I was wondering if you'd be interested in sharing some ideas about writing, exchange stories, or things like that."

I jumped at the opportunity. I wanted to improve my writing skills and craved feedback other than the patronizing "I like it" from friends who didn't want to hurt my feelings. So, I didn't ignore and delete the message as I normally would from a stranger, choosing instead to check out her profile.

She was a gorgeous black woman, with wide, bright eyes and a smile that went on for miles. She looked happy and friendly, like one of those persons you meet for the first time and it feels like you have been friends forever. We had four mutual friends, all Barbadian, so she wasn't a complete stranger and out of my network. I accepted her friend request and we exchanged email addresses and our short stories.

The beginning of our friendship coincided with the end of the relationship with my boyfriend, Jason. We had been together for four years; two of which we spent planning to marry. It was a bad break-up, simply because I felt that Jason not only no longer loved me, but didn't even like me as a person. It only took one word to escape from my mouth to get him angry or annoyed, and sometimes I sat in silence, afraid to say anything in fear of spoiling his good mood. I had to initiate all contact and we had numerous arguments about the little time we spent together. Sometimes, he barely looked at me and when he did, it was with a mixture of disgust and frustration. I never seemed to be able to do anything right. I was inundated with constant criticism of any small task. But the fear of doing something wrong was nothing compared to the fear of doing nothing at all, and risking a stare of disappointment.

I reached my breaking point after we met to talk about our relationship, and it somehow turned into an hour-long attack about my flaws and why I needed to change. Through my tears, I asked him what his flaws were, and he said, "Putting up with yours".

Just like nearing the end of a toothpaste tube, Jason and I dragged out our breakup for as long as possible. We still chatted and emailed everyday, mostly to argue, sometimes to cry on the phone or reminisce about the good times; sometimes to talk about a possible reunion with the occasional sex romp to put a flimsy plaster on a wound that clearly required surgery.

All the while, my relationship with Daphne evolved from story editor to friend. She too was going through a breakup with a guy who had left her for another woman. Chatting online we shared our pain and stories, while giving each other advice well into obscene early morning hours. Her friendship came at a time when I had few people to talk to, as I shared most of my friends with Jason and they felt uncomfortable having to choose sides.

One day, Daphne messaged that her mother was diagnosed with cervical cancer and didn't have a lot of time to live. Hearing about her problems made mine seem so trivial. She had to deal with a dying parent and an ex who not only insisted on being a part of her mother's remaining days on earth, but also wanted Daphne's mom to get to know his new girlfriend before she went to heaven.

I remembered one of the saddest opening lines from Daphne's email: "The strangest feeling in the world must be to plan your mother's funeral with her." We spent the whole night talking about her problems and getting even closer. She sent me pictures of her whole family: her mom, sister and niece, and they all had the same bright eyes and wide smile. I shed a little tear at the thought that death had decided to kiss someone so undeserving of it. Those tears quickly dried up when Daphne sent me a picture of her highly insensitive ex-boyfriend.

In the meantime, Jason and I were cordial to each other, which at the time seemed refreshing since we were always at each other's throats. Against my instincts, I started to daydream about us getting back together and following through with our wedding plans.

When I first met Jason, he seemed like the perfect guy. He was very attractive, an extremely popular and talented entertainer, more open-minded than any man I knew and very sensitive. He knew how to make me feel special with gifts, specially-written songs and poems and told me how beautiful I was every day.

And the sex was phenomenal. Too phenomenal.

We spent little time actually talking in the relationship, and every problem was solved with his face between my legs. Days of silence and not discussing feelings ended only when we became too sexually frustrated, and our problems hit the floor next to our torn clothing. Obviously with nothing solved, the issues would resurface as soon as the afterglow faded.

With Jason being as popular and good-looking as he was, our relationship was plagued with giggly girls hoping to score one night with him. Due to his career, he had to interact with plenty of women who flung themselves at him continuously, sometimes even stripping in front of him, hoping to tempt him away from me.

At least that's what he told me.

So, it was my duty as a girlfriend to troll his Facebook page for any homewrecker that got out of hand and reinstating my authority as girlfriend by being the first to comment on his every post with love statuses as well as numerous kissy-face pictures. I made sure he was tagged so that they could see that he was in a happy relationship and not interested in any of them.

Then Lisa appeared.

Jason told me Lisa worked with him on a project, and their relationship was strictly professional. Yet I found that Lisa managed to "like" and comment on his statuses even before I did! What sort of woman sat waiting by a computer for his alerts and updates? I brought it up with Jason, and he said that she works online, and probably had a small crush on him and we laughed together at her pathetic and overzealous behaviour.

But still, I became obsessed with Lisa, tracking her Facebook posts and getting to know more about her business and personal life. I was jealous. She seemed nice, talented and successful - a better version of me. She even had a degree in a topic I was very interested in. The year before I had seen a brochure for the programme and excitedly called Jason, telling him that I wanted to apply for the school. Jason informed me that it was a great opportunity, but there was no way he would have a long distance relationship and we would have to break up. I chose to stay in the island, and researched various online programmes, but never found one similar to that one-year programme in the United States.

I also realized that our mutual friends were increasing. It seemed as if she was befriending as many of Jason's friends as possible. In fact, one friend commented that Lisa had approached the group in a nightclub, and was so nice and friendly they all embraced her. Jason claimed that he didn't know she was going to be there, and it would have been rude to have her standing there and not introduce her.

I was becoming more and more suspicious by the minute. One day, Lisa opened a Twitter account and sent a tweet to Jason. This wouldn't have been anything out of the ordinary, except that I didn't know he had a Twitter account! When I called him, furious, he claimed he opened the account an hour ago and was about to follow me, and didn't know how Lisa found out about his account so quickly.

Soon Jason sat me down and called an intervention. He told me that I was obsessed with Lisa and was becoming as crazy as she was. By the time we were finished, I was so upset about my insecurity and low self-esteem I decided to ignore everything Lisa did, since it caused strife in our relationship.

Imagine how I felt then, while in the middle of a daydream of Jason and I getting back together, someone mentioned that they saw Jason and Lisa in the nightclub and Lisa was all over him.

I was so angry. She leapt at the opportunity to get

with him as soon as we were done. My first thought was to call Jason immediately to reconcile. I could not bear the thought of him and Lisa together, but I followed my second instinct and went online to message Daphne.

Daphne was even more furious than I was. I remember being a little surprised by the level of her anger as the exclamation marks and capital letters came up on screen. She advised me to leave Jason alone and to move on with my life, and she convinced me that it was for the best. She even offered to send me money via Western Union so I would not even have to contact him about returning a small loan I had given him.

Jason did not react well to my silence.

He sent me multiple emails and texts, asking why I was ignoring him. Every message chipped away at my resistance, so that when he sent me an email begging for us to meet and talk, I wanted nothing more than to go. I went online and told Daphne that I was planning to meet him, and that is when she cracked.

She begged me not to go. Daphne had done some research on Jason and Lisa. She only knew one other person in Barbados, other than her direct family, and that person happened to be good friends with Lisa.

Daphne was informed that not only were Jason and Lisa in a relationship, but they had been in one for several months before I knew Lisa existed. I didn't believe Daphne at first, but then she started to get specific, telling me details about events where Jason had disappeared to meet up with Lisa, about the times he used my car to drive to her house in the North - she even recited my license plate number! Jason told Lisa he was in love with both of us and could not choose. She patiently waited as the outside woman, anticipating the day Jason would choose her.

Daphne begged me to forgive her for snooping, and not to go do anything stupid. She knew about the affair for weeks, but did not bother to tell me about it since she thought that I was done with Jason and wanted to spare me the pain.

I sat in silence, watching the words come up on the screen. Surprisingly, I didn't immediately feel pain, or hurt, or anger…but relief. I guess a part of me knew Lisa could not have just been a friend, but did not want to admit it. Knowing that Jason had not only lied, but also made me feel like I was crazy, made it a lot easier to move on. I wrote him one last long email, telling him that I had found out about the affair, articulately described what I thought of him and never spoke to him again.

Most men who are caught in a lie normally are ashamed, and try to apologise, but not Jason.

He was furious.

He told all of our mutual friends various lies as to why we broke up and how vindictive I was, and that I was stalking his friends. He had no idea how I found out the details about Lisa and assumed Lisa's only mutual friend with me must have spilled the beans. He launched an attack on that friend's character as well. One by one I saw how people who I thought were my friends turn against me, spread the rumours and gave me disgusted looks whenever they saw me.

I remained silent, never once defending myself. Those who chose to speak to me about the rumours instead of spreading them were put on a fresh list of genuine friends. I still didn't tell them what had happened, but assured them that the vindictive things that were being said were not true.

As a public figure, Jason made our break-up situation more public, writing several harsh Facebook statuses and poems about our relationship. It is the strangest and most horrible feeling to watch hundreds of people who know nothing about you comment about you and your life and making disparaging remarks about your character.

Daphne and my best friend Jenna were there for me through it all. They kept me sane through that hurtful period and helped me to heal. I really appreciated Daphne's attention to me, especially since her mother had permanently been moved to the hospital by then.

A few weeks later, Jenna and I were talking about the situation and commented on how coincidental it was that Daphne happened to know Lisa's close friend.

"Have you ever met Daphne?" she asked.

I realized I hadn't.

Social media had encompassed my relationship and social structure so much, that I could forge deep friendships with someone I never met. I had never even heard Daphne's voice.

I immediately messaged her online and asked if we could chat on Skype or on the phone. She replied that she was really emotional, but would download Skype so we could talk. Her mother had officially gone into a coma, and the doctors didn't think she was going to wake up.

Days passed and I didn't hear from her, and I sent her an email asking for an update. The email bounced back, with the message: "the delivery to the following participant has failed permanently. The email account that you tried to access does not exist."

Confused, I tried to message Daphne on Facebook, but her profile was gone. I messaged our four mutual friends – all male – in a panic, asking each of them if they had contact information for her.

Three of them told me that she had sent them friend requests on Facebook but only added Daphne because she was pretty. The remaining mutual friend said she used to go to martial arts training with him a couple years back. None of them knew anything more about her or how to contact her.

I never heard from Daphne again.

Years later, my friends and I still debate about if she was real. Some argue that the trauma of her Mom dying caused her to reject all social media. We speculate that maybe Daphne was a mutual friend of Jason and mine who knew all that he was doing to me and wanted to find a way to intervene without betraying his trust. I still wonder if Daphne was actually Lisa, who befriended me on Facebook to try to ensure that I didn't get back together with Jason.

Everything seemed so implausible.

Who would be determined enough to create a whole life and back story for a person, dying mother included, complete with stock photos? To what end?

I don't know who Daphne was, but you know what? I don't care.

The friendship was real to me, and several times I turned to her when I had no one else to talk to. I would not have survived that break-up if it weren't for her. It is very possible that I would have gotten back into that horrible relationship with Jason had Daphne not told me about Jason's infidelity - something that various friends didn't have the courage to do. I had some tough lessons to learn too - one of them being the over-dependence on social media. Now I am a very private person, putting nothing personal on Facebook, and valuing telephone calls and face-to-face interactions over pokes and tweets.

I think that Daphne, real or fake, is still out there watching me. Maybe she will read this story. I want to tell her thank you, and that I miss her very much. Whenever I look back at the unhealthy and emotionally abusive relationship I had with Jason, I shudder to think about how stunted my development as a person and a professional would have been if I had remained with him.

I want to tell Daphne that no matter who she is or was, that I don't call her a freak, a fraud, or a crazy person, but I smile and look to the sky with gratitude, and think of her as my Guardian Angel.

Daphne, the next time you see me, please say hello.

EMBRACING THE TABOO

Red Redemption
Annia Bryce

I waited as long as I could for sweet redemption.

Sitting on the cusp of seventeen, I carefully prepared myself and my tiny bedroom as a shrine of sacrifice in the heat of an otherwise blue Barbadian summer.

"Are you sure you want to do this?" whispered my boyfriend.

He was twelve years my senior and scared of hurting the nervous teenager lying underneath his skinny caramel body, toned by years of tinkering with cars.

"Yes, I'm ready."

I am not exactly sure if I really meant it but I said it anyway. I was too curious; I wanted to know what it felt like to have that tingle tangoed, touched and poked at, stroked and caressed.

*****

Weekly church attendance was non-negotiable in my extended family. Christian Way was built forty years ago by a group of newly-baptized Christians after a crusade swept through eastern Christ Church. The band of fifteen packed their families onto the holy train and added to its carriages through births and marriages. A few of the founding fathers and mothers still rule the small, white and blue concrete house of prayer and quiet praise - firmly ensuring the traditional values of decades past remained intact.

A simple church, the decorations have always been minimal: a white plastic vase with fake pink and white flowers adorned the pulpit, while a crimson runner led sinners to the altar. Wooden pews were re-varnished every couple years, as were the white metal burglar bars aimed at keeping the undesirables out in a once volatile neighbourhood.

Clapping, dancing or loud outbursts of praise were not tolerated under any circumstances, and the order of service was exactly the same week after week: singing started promptly at 9:15 a.m. and the preacher mounted the platform no later than 11:30. He (in rare cases, she) was given an hour before older members huffily exited through a side door.

Shifting uncomfortably in my pew on that Sunday after my sin, it felt as though the pastor knew what I had done. He pointed his sweaty, judgment-laden finger between my eyes while condemning me and the "homosexuals, drunkards, idolaters and pleasure-seekers" to the same fiery fate.

My heart sank.

I was not exactly sure what heaven *was*, but was pretty certain I wanted to go. I memorised my fair share of Bible verses, was an active member of youth group and encouraged my friends to go to church. I could not allow this one thing to get in the way of my "wholeness".

As I closed my eyes for the prayer of consecration, hot flashes of a vision stung my eyes: I was standing in a line, waiting to be judged by Jesus. He wore a white robe with a blue sash slung from his right shoulder. Light brown hair cascaded to his neck. Blue eyes twinkled beneath a halo.

My sister was in front of me, followed by my mother

and grandmother. Soon, it was my turn.

I was excited to see the Man I had heard and read and sang about, the One who would forgive me and usher me beyond mysterious pearly white gates.

"Depart from Me. You fornicated!"

"But...I...It was just the one time, and I was really sorry about it...I...uh..."

"You WHAT?" my mother screamed, staring at me with eyes dazed by shock, shame and sadness.

My grandmother starts to cry, but shouts of my sister's "I told you so's" drown her tears.

Everything fades to black. Then red. Black again. Orange fire flickers and rises.

I think I am in hell.

The prayer was over, but I was still standing. I resolved never to allow myself to fall prey to the Devil who feverishly sought to devour my righteousness and transform me into a made-up, high-heeled, slutty Jezebel. Sex hurt too much anyway. "Something that painful isn't worth spending eternity in a burning pit," I reasoned.

I told Tony about the new resolve a few days later.

"Why? Didn't it feel good?"

"Well, Jesus doesn't like fornication. I will go to hell for this," I responded, reciting my prearranged answer.

"Oh..." Anthony's eyes fell to his hands.

"We could do other stuff," I added quickly. "I could suck your... thing... and you could finger me or whatever...."

Shit.

I didn't want Tony to think I was an immature teenager who couldn't handle the emotions of sex, especially since I was the youngest girlfriend he'd ever had. I leaned over to kiss him on the lips, as a sign of my coolness and maturity.

In five minutes we were spread-eagled on my mother's favourite mahogany chair. As horny as Tony was, he was twice as respectful and we stopped before the kisses could escalate.

We decided to be celibate. It was hard…well his penis was, but good old Christian guilt would creep up on me, and just like that little white angel that pops up on people's shoulder in the movies, my conscience would remind me of the fire and brimstone waiting to roast my ass for all eternity.

A few months later, Tony and I celebrated our first Valentine's Day as a couple. Never one for sweeping romantic gestures, my boyfriend dropped a large white teddy bear on my lap as soon as I got into his too-bright yellow Mazda and gave me a kiss.

"Love ya, boo," he said with his uniquely childish smile.

On our drive along the south coast, we held hands, stole kisses by red lights, shared laughs and "I love yous". As the night wore on, Tony parked the car and kisses became even more intense and passionate. Tony slipped his hand under my grey skirt, slowly moving towards my eager vagina. Desperately yearning for the closeness we shared so many months before, I flicked that little bitch off my shoulder, straight through the window and right into the Caribbean Sea.

I unzipped his oversized Fat Albert jeans, pushed past his boxers and gently rubbed his dick as I tried to stabilise my feet, which kept hitting against the gearstick and lodging between the seats.

The feeling of his penis growing in my hand made

me giddy with pleasure.

I held him closer as I straddled his skinny frame. I shifted my thong. He pulled down his pants a little, fumbling to quickly put on a condom. With his help, I carefully positioned myself on top of his throbbing cock.

Oh....my....

god?

I had never felt so liberated.

But, WWJD???

Not this, that I knew. For the Bible told me so.

*****

Tony and I stayed together for a few months after that night. I got tired of the constant job complaints but lacking the drive to do anything about it. All these years later, there is still a place in my heart for him, even though I am not sorry about moving on.

But I had been pricked. My blood boiled to the surface, tainting the white robes of virginal sanctification. I could go back and beg the Lord to wash my raiment, make it white as snow again, but I didn't want to.

I wanted to fuck, but the angry Jesus of my dreams would come flashing back, and I would spend days on end asking for forgiveness, reciting the most recent "epiphany" about my body belonging to the Lord. Just as soon as I got up off my knees, I sank to them just as easily to provide deep-throated pleasure to whoever was into me at the time.

"Maybe I should talk to someone...." I told myself after a particularly distasteful sexual rendezvous with a fun-sized medical student I was screwing out of self-pity.

I confided in the resident advisor on my dormitory. Tall and gentle, he was eager to listen and pray. He encouraged me to be safe, if not careful, and promised to keep asking God to help me.

I tried my best to follow his guidance but I slipped constantly. The battle between the desires of my body and the teachings of the Word of God tore my mind to shreds. I allowed a kaleidoscope of men into my sacred sanctuary, and with every sting of relationship gone awry or casual fling which dissolved into a pillow full of tears, I would ask for forgiveness again for my whoring ways.

For a time, I thought it was working. I paid more attention to church, lent my talents to youth groups and read the Bible during my down time. In repressing my sexual feelings, I thought it best to find a good Christian boy who wanted the same things I wanted, forming a relationship that would lead down the aisle.

Larry was that boy.

To be honest, the Jamaican was not my type. He was a little rude and wore chauvinism proudly. But we were both of the same denomination, so I gave in to his relentless pursuit and entered a relationship.

By the end of the first week, Larry and I had had sex three times, mostly in the afternoon when my roommate was at class. We kept up the appearances of an upright Christian couple even though we were at it whenever we could steal the chance. We would make out in the shadows of midnight at youth retreats in central Jamaican hills. Secret hand-jobs were given while our counterparts slept through a three-hour bus ride to a small village on the outskirts of Kingston.

I dumped him on hi5 on my summer back home, and my internal struggle continued with another man from another place.

Still, I longed to find answers in my faith. I wanted

Jesus to erase my scarlet A. But as I got older, I realised there were too many things conventional Christianity did not solve. Every question begged another - and no answers other but to look to a Deity I did not really understand. I was never really sure if God was talking to me in my prayers, or if it was just my conscience playing tricks.

*****

Time has passed.

Most of the friends I once shared these thoughts with are either pregnant or taking their kids to school.

From time to time, I revisit the Christian Way. Faint traces of slight nostalgia run though me whenever I see the varnished wooden pews of my childhood. Maybe it will change with time.

For now, I choose sex, and fucking has become my religion. I lay prostrate at its feet.

In its presence, all is forgiven and the moment is enjoyed.

Selah

The Younger Man
Maymar Johnson

When people look at me, they never think that I am the type that would enjoy sex, or even know what passion feels like. But I do, and I have.

Now that I'm in my forties and have been in a relationship for the past eleven years, I sometimes find myself looking back and recalling past encounters. Some were so painful I wanted to die. Another was abusive…I won't go into that one…you understand. But there's one in particular that I will never forget, and when I say those words I often add the phrase "even when I become old and toothless". For once in my life I dared to experience forbidden fruit. Some women consider it a taboo, while some men look at it as a rite of passage. Call it whatever you will, but to me he was deliciously sweet fruit I wanted to savour from the very first day I saw him enter my art class.

You're probably thinking that I was the teacher - I wasn't. I was one of thirty students honing my artistic talents at one of Trinidad and Tobago's tertiary institutions. At thirty-three, I was an anomaly. Nearly everyone else was in their early twenties or fresh out of secondary school. Other than that, we were all the same: gifted, hungry and competitive.

Our teachers lectured on art history and handed out assignments. We submitted our work, took our various critiques and accepted our grades. Exams were especially brutal and by the second semester, the class was whittled down to eleven students.

And on the first day of the new semester, we got another.

His name was Brent.

He was all of 5' 5", with a light caramel brown complexion and an average build. He had sweet, pert lips that sat above a goatee. He walked in the room before class began, carrying his giant sketch pad and knapsack over one shoulder.

Amber-coloured eyes locked onto my smile and mouthed the words, "I could sit next to you?"

I nodded yes.

For a moment I forgot where I was and I let myself get lost in him, watching him stride over to my table and place his things on it and taking up residence in the no longer empty chair.

"We ent start yet, right?" he asked.

"No, not yet," I said. "It still has a couple of minutes before Miss comes."

"Great." And he was gone, no doubt to find the cafeteria, as the other students often did. He came back with arms were laden with snacks.

"I didn't eat lunch."

He smiled when he saw the look on my face.

"Hope you have a fast metabolism," I countered.

"Actually I do," he replied, opening a pack of Kiss cupcakes.

"Want one?"

"Why not…I didn't eat lunch either."

I soon learned his name and that he was from Diego Martin. He went to the same secondary school my young son was now attending after passing his SEA exams. He had a part-time job at the phone company and shared an apartment with one of his UWI friends. His parents worked in the energy sector and had only just given him a new car for his 19th birthday a couple of months ago.

Nineteen.

I suddenly felt old sitting next to him…I don't know why. Maybe subconsciously I was hoping we had more in common than the classroom. He was exactly my type, despite his height. I never really liked men that were too tall. Besides, everyone was the same height in bed.

I remember going through the rest of the class doing my best to shut him out from my brain, but the devil was working overtime somehow, because Brent found every conceivable way to make his presence felt, from borrowing my eraser to sharing my notes.

Next thing I knew, the lecturer was giving out our drawing assignments for the weekend. We were to pair off and draw each other, using an assigned medium. Just as I was about to ask my usual partner Jessica to team up with me, the lecturer said we would be paired off with the person we sat next to.

The vexing chorus of irritated protests will forever be etched in my mind. Secretly, I was angry, but then the feeling changed to one of intrigue.

I felt a touch on my shoulder.

"I think we got the best out of that deal," a cheeky Brent whispered.

Was this boy reading my mind?

"Seriously?" I replied.

"How you mean? Out of everyone in this class, I think we have the best bodies here. I can't wait to draw yours." Before I could answer, we heard our names.

"Brent Hinkson: chalk pastels."

"Natasha Lyons: charcoal."

"Thank you Jesus," I whispered, writing down my assignment.

"Wait, wait…Tasha, why are you so happy to get charcoal?"

"It's my favourite medium," I said. "And I don't think I gave you permission to call me Tasha."

He gave a mocking grin. "We are going to be drawing each other in a state of undress in a day or two. The way I see it, the more familiar we get now, the less stressful it will be later, you know? So let's relax. When do you want to start work on it?"

Mentally, I checked my calendar. My son would be at his grandmother's for the weekend. I would be all alone.

"Saturday?"

"Cool. What time so? For that matter, what is your address?"

"We can't do it by you instead?" I asked hopefully.

"Nah, I have a roommate and I think the sight of you would make him not want to leave us alone," he said with a huge grin.

"So you want to get me alone?" I grinned.

His voice deepened. "Nutten wrong in that."

Again I was intrigued. This youngster was tracking! Suddenly, I didn't feel so old anymore as I wrote my address down in his notebook.

"Be there after lunch."

"See you then, Tasha."

***

Brent had arrived right on time, just as I had finished setting up my easel. I remember dressing simply in a shirt that buttoned down the front and paired it with a short skirt. Underneath, I wore a sports bra and biker shorts. He came dressed in blue jeans, slippers and a polo shirt, carrying the usual backpack and 18x24 inch sketch pad. I offered him a beer. We talked shop for a little, then soon got down to the business of drawing, flipping a coin to see who would pose first; I lost the toss.

I shed my clothing without a second thought, grabbed the sheet I had set up and turned my back to him.

"Where do you want me?" I said casually.

When he looked up, he gasped. My breasts were hidden, but knowing that I was naked under there...I knew he was secretly thrilled. So was I, actually. There is something about showing yourself off to another human being that I find absolutely intoxicating.

He tied the sheet around my waist and made me touch my right hand on my left shoulder. My eyes looked left, and my left hand was placed on my waist.

"I know it's not an easy pose to hold, but bear with me," he whispered hotly.

He worked quickly. Preliminary sketches were done in no time and the filling in went without a hitch.

"You want to see?"

Grabbing my sheet, I walked over to his canvas, where I saw myself staring back at me, looking like a Grecian goddess.

Damn, I thought. *He's good. I have got to bring my "A" game.*

I put my clothing back on, sans the sports bra. We changed positions. He quickly doffed his clothing and picked up the sheet to wrap it around his lower half.

"How do you want me?"

I looked up from my easel and saw a perfectly chiselled six-pack that supported a beautifully smooth chest, shoulders and arms. He seemed to be all muscle. His nipples were a beautiful cherry brown. Unconsciously, I licked my lips, and something in the air felt different, like an electric charge of some sort.

"Wait," I said. I went to the other room to retrieve a chair.

"Sit facing the back of the chair," I told him. "I'll fix the sheet."

I wanted to capture his beautifully chiselled back muscles and shoulders. The sheet was draped around the front of his waist, leaving his buttocks exposed. He leaned forward to rest his head in his arms.

Charcoal sticks in hand, I worked, concentrating only on the network of muscles I saw in front of me. And as it always happens when I'm drawing live nudes, my brain took flight and made my hands move to bring my creation to life. My fingertips traced the outline of his spine, the gluteal muscles and the dimples above them. I shaded, moved from light to dark. I captured shadow and sinew. I drew him as a loving creator would. In the end, I had captured him perfectly.

"Come see," I said.

I wiped my fingers on a small wet rag, glad that it was finally over. Inwardly, I was spent, yet I was suddenly aware of him next to me, looking at the drawing I had done of him. He was so close to me, I could inhale his scent. I slowly closed my eyes, hoping he wouldn't realise how much my body was reacting.

"You really captured me, Tasha."

"I had a good subject to work with."

I felt his hand encircle my waist as we stood side by side.

"So did I," he said.

I didn't want to look at him, because I knew that he knew I was becoming aroused.

The feeling was intoxicating.

I could feel his eyes on me, waiting…wanting…

"It's okay," I heard him say, his breath warm on my ear.

I slowly turned to face him and kept my eyes closed. I knew that if I looked him in the eye, common sense would win and I would have likely scolded him for being too forward. So I kept them closed and inhaled his sweet scent of young lust.

His hand encircled my waist, and just like that, he was holding me close and pressing his lips to my own, and his tongue, still tasting of the Spearmint gum he had been chewing, entered my parted lips to seek mine and taste mine…

I kissed him back, because he kissed me the way I wanted to be kissed, with soft, yielding lips and a tongue that knew exactly how much pressure was needed to titillate and tease his willing mouth.

And we stood there, fascinated by the fierce sweetness of that first kiss.

"My God, what are we doing?" I heard myself ask him.

He answered me with another sweet, deep kiss that left me breathless.

"No, Brent. We can't do this. I can't do this. You're still a teenager…this is wrong…we can't…we can't…"

But his lips and tongue continued their assault on my senses, and I was powerless to stop. I let his hands open the top three buttons of my shirt and I could feel his fingertips on my breasts, and my nipples were being gently touched and caressed between his long fingers. I let myself enjoy what he was doing to my body and the feeling travelled all the way to my stiffening clitoris.

He opened my shirt and moved me to the wall, gently raising my arms over my head. He kissed my neck and his tongue made a gentle trail to the centre of my chest. When he finally took my left nipple into his mouth, I moaned my gratitude. His mouth created a gentle suction that reminded me of when I was nursing my son as a baby and unconsciously I placed my hand underneath my breast so he could take the entire nipple, areola and all, into his mouth. He repeated the action on my right nipple; I loved it so.

He stopped to remove the sheet, and this time I could finally touch the body that I had only previously committed to paper in charcoal. I could place my hands on his chest, and hug him, and feel his heart beating strongly against my body. I let my hands explore the muscles on his back. I touched and played with his nipples, kissing and nuzzling them gently with my lips and tongue and watching him smile. I looked into his eyes as I opened the sheet to put my hand on his hard cock.

"Take it."

"No, not yet," I said, and I took his hand. "Let's go to my room."

"Wait, you have a CD player in there?"

"Yes. Why?"

He smiled, and walked over to his backpack and pulled out a CD.

"It's something special, for us."

And he took my hand and followed me on bare feet as I led him into my bedroom, and locked the door behind me.

He sat on my bed and stared at me in my state of undress.

"You know, you have no idea how sexy you look to me right now," he said, licking his lips.

I couldn't help but blush.

"Put this in," he said, handing me the CD. I placed it in my player and closed it with the remote. Scandalous by Prince crooned through the speakers.

"Well played, Mr. Hinkson."

He smiled.

"Glad you approve. Now why don't you take your clothes off for me?"

I obeyed, sliding my shirt off my shoulders and letting it drop to the floor. My skirt and panty soon followed, and everything lay in a colourful puddle at my feet.

His eyes took me in from head to painted toe. He walked over to me and it took everything I had to maintain my composure.

"I want to see you," I heard myself saying in his ear. "All of you."

He smiled as he dropped the sheet.

And at that precise moment in time as we stood there facing each other, I realised that this was as honest as we were ever going to be. Our age difference no longer mattered. We were two consenting adults about to make love. No more pretence. No beating around the bush. No fear.

As I looked into his eyes, I no longer saw a nineteen year-old youth. I saw a young man that was sure of himself.

A man that understood his lust for me, and mine for him.

I opened myself up to him and covered his willing mouth with mine in a passionate kiss. He held me tightly, his hands moving all over my back and buttocks.

My body responded to his touch; his kisses became even more intense. I found myself grinding my lower half against his pelvis, enjoying how he stiffened against my crotch.

We slowly wined to the music of Prince and I slid his hand between my legs to feel my clit, wet and slick with arousal. He dropped to his knees and positioned me on the edge of the bed. I lay back and felt his thumb gently press against my clitoris, moving the hood deliciously up and down. I felt his lips on the inside of my thighs, and they came closer and closer...his hand gently spread my labia and his lips and tongue went to work on my eager pussy...

Licking...

Sucking...

Nuzzling...

Tasting...

My hands were on my stiffening nipples, making them come to attention, stopping only to touch his head as he buried his lips in my wetness. I wanted him inside me so badly.

I don't even remember how we both ended up in bed, but somehow we were lying belly to belly and I was guiding him to enter me. My legs were spread wide and the tip of his cock was at the entrance to my deliciously wet snatch. He bent his head to suck on my nipples again, and with all this sweet torture I could only imagine how it would feel when he entered me. I grabbed his firm ass and locked my legs into his and wined against him hard, and gasped with delight when I felt him enter me.

I was holding him like a hot wet fist between my legs, and feeling wanton as he slid in and out, in and out…I could feel him through my entire body.

I felt like he belonged to me and I belonged to him.

His movements increased and the slapping of our bodies together was too much for me.

I let him turn me on my belly. He grabbed on to my waist to steady himself and started fucking me again, this time harder…faster…the feeling reached all the way to my trembling belly. His scrotum rudely slapped against my cunt with each thrust, bringing me closer and closer to orgasm. I heard him inhale sharply…his breathing changed, growing ragged and raspy as he finally let go, and came in a furious climax, emptying his balls into my quim.

A feeling of sweetness spread through my lower half, making my hips rise and buck against him, and I screamed my own orgasm a few seconds later.

We spent the evening making love, over and over again, and that sweet memory of him has been burned into my brain forever. Wherever he is now, I like to think that sometimes he remembers me and that magical day we each embraced our taboo.

The Driveway
N.Dee

It was half past four in the a.m. and they were headed to Lookout, again. A clandestine location in the hills of upper St. Andrew had become their regular spot in recent months.

It was summer and the weekends were particularly hot, with at least two parties being held each night. This Friday, Appleton was getting adolescents drunk at the Mas Camp on Oxford Road while Smirnoff was doing the same at the Jonkunnu Lounge in New Kingston. They were both there, at separate times, for work. In fact, working in the entertainment industry is what got them together in the first place.

The first time he laid eyes on her, she was dancing seductively, swaying to the beat of the music in the middle of the dance floor. She was completely carefree. He was mesmerized by her moves. He wanted to be wherever she was. He told her all this when they finally met by the sound system later that night. It was during these initial introductions that her friend, who had met him previously and was currently under the influence of something strong with lime, announced that he was off limits.

"You know what *this* means right?" she shouted over the speakers, holding up his hand and brandishing his wedding band. He was like a deer caught in headlights.

The revelation crushed her. It had been quite some

time since she truly appreciated the company of a man, and the way he licked his lips and stared deep into her eyes made her want to explore his every fantasy.

But thanks to the alcohol, and despite the "warning" from her friend, she gave him her number when asked and dismissed the band around his finger.

Six months later, here they were: climbing the hill towards their secret hideaway. It seemed they weren't the only ones feeling the heat that night. When they arrived there was no space. Seeing the congestion, he took a sharp left turn and began to climb the hill towards the more residential area. They passed rows and rows of perfect family homes, which were only missing the white picket fences. Meanwhile, she quietly pondered on the certainty of his navigation until he pulled up in front of a large green gate and jumped out of the car to open it. Where were they? What was he doing?

Still tipsy from the night of drinking and revelry, she didn't have the energy to get into an argument about their whereabouts, especially since he offered no explanation.

He pulled into the driveway and switched off the engine. Minutes passed as he fiddled with the radio tuner and adjusted his seat - pushing it all the way back.

"So..." she sighed, turning to face him while taking in her new surroundings. Even though outside was dark, she was still able to make out a two-toned, three-storey house with a fountain in the front garden and a Fisher Price bike in the garage.

Before she could begin her inquisition, his tongue was in her mouth and hand up her skirt, tugging at her thong. She let out a sweet moan as she circled her tongue around his, then sucked on his bottom lip. She loved the way he tasted like double mint gum.

She had worn a mini skirt and a tube top for this exact reason - easy off, easy on. He dragged down her top to reveal two robust breasts, round and juicy like ripe Bombay mangoes. He held them both firmly in his hands and slowly massaged them as he ran his tongue from behind her ears to her left nipple, circling it, then heading to the right. Throwing her head back, she groped around his pants in the dark until she found it - already stiff and begging to be released from its denim prison. She pulled the zipper and out it popped, in all its hooked glory.

She smiled as she felt it pulsating in her hands; it was thick and warm. Meanwhile, he was busy leaving his mark on her left breast. He had a way of applying just enough pressure for it to feel damn good and not as if she was being attacked by Dracula. The way he sucked then flicked his tongue over her nipples was like a work of art. She was flooded and he knew it.

He whispered in her ear, "I wanna taste you now", as he removed her lace thong and hung it on the rear-view mirror, gently massaging her tender flower in the process. Instantly she melted.

His hunger for her was normally insatiable, but tonight he was feeling particularly experimental. Regardless of the fact that they were about to "do the deed" in his wife's car again, he seemed particularly intrigued by their current positioning in a random driveway. He turned her upside down so her legs hung over the back of the seat. She giggled as the blood simultaneously rushed to her head and clitoris. Spreading her legs apart, he reclined her seat to an obtuse angle so he could properly bury his face between her legs.

She closed her eyes and tried to steady herself, bracing her hands on the door. She could feel her first orgasm travel to her groin, as she tried to keep her legs from trembling. He grabbed her thighs to keep her from escaping while keeping one eye outside. But she was too busy floating past stars to notice his preoccupation with the great outdoors. She was ready for the dick. She wanted it and she wanted it NOW. Addicted, she loved the way his dick looked, its shape and the curve of the head. She had even taken to having small conversations with it, kissing and rubbing its head, licking it tenderly. She loved its texture, its taste, its smell. She was completely and utterly smitten with his dick. That's when she knew she was in too deep. Because now it was all she could think about - that beautiful curved dick.

And that's all she was thinking about that night in the driveway as she kissed and caressed its head, licking it from the base up to the stem. She thought about just how happy her pussy would be once this dick was finally inside her.

He was back in his seat, pants at his ankles as she straddled him and carefully slid his dick into her. She was moist and warm and the walls of her pussy clenched as he sank deeper and deeper inside her. His eyes rolled back into his head as she began her slow clockwise rotation on his cock, speeding up at every 32 beats. He grabbed her breasts and began to knead them as she switched to a back and forth rocking motion. She threw her head back as she moved to the beat of the song playing on the radio. How appropriate, R. Kelly's Bump and Grind.

The buddy head rubbing on her g-spot was becoming too much for her to bear. She clutched the back of the chair and prepared for the great arrival. Her quick contractions on his dick triggered his own reaction and they came almost concurrently, as she buried her face into his chest screaming unintelligible expletives.

After their heart rates had returned to normal and they were detached from each other, she sat back into the passenger seat still breathing heavily, but basking in the endorphins, which were now surging throughout her body.

She glanced at the clock.

It was almost 6 a.m., which meant the sun would be rising in a few minutes. She still had no idea where she was. It was probably one of the best orgasms she'd had in a while but now that the buzz was wearing off, she was becoming concerned that they had committed some kind of offence. Whose house was this? Why did he carry her here?

Then she saw a light on the top floor go on. Apparently he did too, because, before she could even blink, he was out the car fixing his pants and heading into the house.

"What the fuck?!?!?" she thought to herself.

Just as she was about to step out of the car and flee, he emerged from the house with a towel in one hand and a glass of water in the other. Opening the car door, he handed the glass to her and switched on the car. Her eyes widened and her mouth was agape with bewilderment.

He simply shot her a sly grin.

"That was amazing!" he whispered, kissing her on the cheek.

She was left speechless as he backed out of the driveway, the morning sun peeking out over the horizon. Kingston was just beginning to stir as she returned home with her thong balled up in her hands and her pride splattered in his driveway.

The Older Man
T. Inniss

What do we call an older man who dates a younger girl?

A dutty ole man.

What do we call a younger woman who dates an older man?

A gold digger.

What do we call a Dark Skinned younger girl who dates a Fair skinned older man?

A dutty black girl.

Society has its own misconstrued definition of older and younger people having intimate relationships. Quite often both parties are ridiculed, and, having been in this situation for over four years, I have learned how to take those criticisms and turn them into stories.

Growing up in an extended family of staunch Jehovah's Witnesses, there were certain things that you could not do or say. My grandmother insisted that Tuesday's book study and Sunday's meeting were not to be missed.

As I grew older, I questioned if I wanted to be forced to worship God or do it on my own. As the years drifted by, I grew apart from my religion, although not away from God and my freedom - or so I called it - became closer and closer.

Even though I was away from meetings, I remained humble in Jehovah's teachings. I decided to join theatre after I left school since it was something I have always told myself I would never do. I challenged myself to find out what it was that made me NOT want to be in theatre.

Had you asked me six years ago: "Do you see yourself dating a man thirty-seven years your senior?" My honest opinion would have been NO, until four years ago, I chose to commit to an older man; we will call him Timothy. He was a smooth talker, quite conversational and a prominent figure in society. We worked on several projects before we decided to make our relationship official.

I was now making a name for myself, now in my fledgling stages and he was my backbone, the one who quite often pushed me to the limit. After months of unsure flirting, we decided to let the cat out of the bag.

"Oh how cute!"

"Really?"

"That's great, Are you sure?" were the sudden outbursts from my friends.

"Yuh joking right?" his friends asked. "You need a young blood to prove yuh still got it eh?"

"Ok...Well, I'm happy for you."

We did not care about sarcastic remarks or questions; we were in it for love.

Because he was well known, I had to survive the several "big shot" events. The glare I got every time he introduced me as his lady made me scream in inside.

There women who were Timothy's age, some of whom he had dated and those who probably wished he had, made sure I bore the brunt of their displeasure.

I was forced to work with some of them and was picked on. I wasn't invited to many hangouts because of our relationship and my work was left on the back burner because no one could stand working with a "gold digger".

A woman even claimed that I had brashly taken Timothy away from her and resorted to emailing a friend of mine to complain.

"I don't know what he could possibly see in her...all his ex-wives are fair skinned, East Indian women with long hair down their backs..." she wrote. *"Maybe I should tell her boss, because she's embarrassing the Muslim community. She's only after his money, she's a gold digger and nothing good would come of them, just watch and see as soon as she's finishing emptying his bank account, he wouldn't know what hit him...poor fella".*

That day after reading the emails, I sat and cried bitter tears. I was mad at myself for being black. I was living in hate with myself and my complexion.

Why do the boys at school only like her? I'm pretty too, I had often thought to myself during school days.

I was also mad at her for not taking the time to know me before judging me as being the gold digger and mad at him for continuing the friendship with this woman even though he confronted her about the email, and I wanted him to be just as angry as I was with her.

Because of my plainspoken attitude, most of my family chose not to say anything about my relationship with Timothy. I was brushed by cold shoulders whenever his name was brought up and I gave the silent treatment to those who brought him up with negative comments. I have lost friendships, of which I have no regrets, and through this relationship I saw the ignorance of many.

Timothy and I had a somewhat open relationship; we talked about anything. My sense of humor coupled with his wit made us enjoy each other's company. Despite the huge age difference and persons cringing at the sight of us together, we never made public affection look too crude, and those who accepted our relationship enjoyed our company.

The true test came in our third year. I was very involved in the arts and my time with Timothy became shorter. He had a demanding job that took up most of his time as well. This, compounded by Timothy's mounting insecurities and my carefree attitude, left room for suspicions and infidelity.

In January 2013, I caught him in a secluded area with a female friend of mine and my thoughts ran wild: *"How could someone so close look me in the face and lie to me?"*

My emotions were torn. I immediately told Timothy I needed space and the time away from him. Then it hit me - I was using his infidelity to get out of a relationship I knew was not going to last. Don't get me wrong, I loved him and I still do, but I needed to be honest with myself and most importantly, with him. Prior to the incident, I was beginning to drift from Timothy mainly because I was starting to realize there was so much more for me to do before I could even dream of settling down.

The hardest part was actually telling Timothy how I really felt and as usual the questions came: "Are you seeing someone else?" he wanted to know.

I did not have the time for that; I knew I wanted out and I wanted out on a good note. He understood and we remain close friends.

Dating an older person certainly has its drama but half of that drama does not start with the person, it starts with society. Everyone is accustomed to doing things traditionally and when someone decides to live outside of the box, it seems like a big deal to everyone else.

I chose to be with Timothy for various reasons, none of which had anything to do with what everyone thought. It was a decision I made because of how I felt.

Even though many did not agree with me, at the end of the day I was comfortable in embracing that part of me, my skin texture and the taboo.

About the Editors

Juliette Maughan

Caribbean Lifestyle Entrepreneur, Social Development Consultant, Gender Equality Advocate and Founder of Ev-O!-lution, Juliette Maughan has a passion for understanding Caribbean sexuality – especially female sexuality. Senseisha represents one of a number of passion projects that combines her professional advocacy efforts and interests, and one that provides something different to the Caribbean market.

Shakirah Bourne

Shakirah is a Barbadian writer, filmmaker, owner of GetWrite! and Partner in film production company, Bajans In Motion Inc. Her short story collection, In Time of Need, was released in 2013. Her films have brought Barbadian and Caribbean culture to screens worldwide. When she is not writing, she spends most of her time sitting on the beach, thinking about the next story to tell.

www.ingramcontent.com/pod-product-compliance
Lightning Source LLC
Chambersburg PA
CBHW051650040426
42446CB00009B/1065